# VICARIOUS ADVENTURES
## ON THE **RICH COAST**

a travel guide and memoir

Chrissy Gruninger

A *for Harmony* Publication © 2010, 2011, 2014

All Rights Reserved.

Printed in the USA

This book is also available on iBooks.

Cover design by Into-Designs; San Jose, Costa Rica

Photo of author on last page by Rachel Balunsat

This book, or parts thereof, may not be reproduced in any form without permission of the author.

## Living Well Book Collection

An Intentional Life

An Interconnected Life

A Harmonious Life

Nourishing Wisdom

Living Intentionally

Daily Yoga

## Rich Coast Experiences Collection

Vicarious Adventures on the Rich Coast

# Table of Contents

| | |
|---|---:|
| Introduction | 1 |
| Chapter 1: Things to know before you go | 6 |
| Chapter 2: EcoTourism | 25 |
| Chapter 3: Samasati Yoga Retreat, Puerto Viejo | 31 |
| Chapter 4: Nosara, Playa Guiones | 35 |
| Chapter 5: Playa Tamarindo | 44 |
| Chapter 6: Fortuna | 55 |
| Chapter 7: Manuel Antonio-Playa Dominical | 60 |
| Chapter 8: Santa Barbara-Sarchi-Poas | 79 |
| Chapter 9: San Jose-Osa Peninsula-San Jose | 88 |
| Chapter 10: San Jose-Las Juntas de Abangares-Monteverde-Tamarindo-San Jose | 103 |
| Chapter 11: Ocotal-Rincon de la Vieja-Tamarindo | 113 |
| Chapter 12: Nosara-Punta Islita-Canas-Papagayo | 127 |
| Chapter 13: Jicaro Island-Granada, Nicaragua | 139 |
| Chapter 14: Playa Tamarindo-Tenorio-San Jose | 154 |
| Chapter 15: Bocas del Toro, Panamá | 163 |
| Chapter 16: Panamá City, Panamá | 167 |
| Chapter 17: Prelude to Trip 8 | 178 |
| Chapter 18: Liberia – Santa Teresa – Tamarindo | 182 |
| Epilogue | 196 |
| Resources | 198 |

*Muchas Gracias...*

*Nati, Silvia and Maureen*...my dear friends on the Rich Coast who, each in their own way, have come along on my adventures, which in turn helped me create this book and who I am so very grateful for.

*Mike and Matthew*...for over a decade, you have both been my friend, during moments of laughter as well as tears. Thank you for your love and support, especially when some of my trips went a little awry.

*And to mi amor, Troy*...without you, this book would not have been written. You have taught me so much about living in a beautiful, yet simple way. You opened my heart to the possibility of love and joy, in the purest sense. I am so blessed to have you as a part of my life's journey.

The purpose of life
is to live it,
to taste experience
to the utmost,
to reach out eagerly
and without fear
for newer and
richer experience.


Eleanor Roosevelt

*Introduction*

As I sat in my car, driving to work on my first day back from my fourth visit to Costa Rica, I gripped the wheel and asked myself, "What am I doing here?"

This is something that I have asked myself many times. Normally it's a question intended in a philosophical manner similar to, "What is my life's purpose?" Living in Sonoma County, I'd had a lot of similarly themed hippie-like existential discussions. This time though, I was asking myself the question literally: Why am I in my car, driving to work on this 32 degree morning which is 0 degrees Celsius (sounds even worse when I convert it) where the entire Petaluma Valley is covered in a layer of very cold white frost? My hands gripped the wheel even tighter as I continued to drive South on 101, now saying the question out loud, "What am I doing here?"

Just a few days before, I was on a tropical beach drinking a cold beer at sunset.  Rare birds (well, rare for this California girl) flew overhead, the warm sunshine and water radiated through my body as a sloth hung from the tree above me eating his dinner.  As the sun melted into the horizon, I looked out to the ocean where mi amor, Troy, was floating on his board.  To say that I felt misplaced would have been the worst form of understatement.

Many of my friends consider me to be a free spirit.  I like to think of myself as one who takes the road less traveled.  My parents allowed me to watch the movie Pippi Longstocking as a child and it paved the way for my adventurous worldview.  Pippi was resilient, empowered and assertive in her beliefs; always standing up for what she believed to be right.  According to Pippi, life was meant to be lived and adventures were meant to be had.  Also, she had a pet monkey - not that I believe humans should have monkeys as pets - but I do hold a special place in my heart for the wild monkeys in Costa Rica. Though fictional, I learned quite a bit from her adventures, thus prompting me to share my own.

My independent nature, along with a very bad relationship that happened in my early 20's, is what has allowed me to live the life I currently enjoy (i.e. 8 international trips to the same country in 4 years). There are some who think I should settle down, get married, have kids and find a corporate job but I am quite content. I work with good people doing good things in the world. I also have other interests such as writing, photography and health coaching which I pursue on the side. I'm fortunate to have a job where my boss allows me to take these vacations as well as take a day off to photograph a 1,000 year old, old-growth redwood tree or a surf competition where I'm only given twenty-four hours notice to get to the site. I have created a life, which allows me to travel, explore new places and meet people who have enriched my life in countless ways and for that, I am blessed. The only downside is that currently, my love is in Costa Rica and I am not. Albeit few and far between, our moments together have always felt natural and I can't help but wonder if he's my true love; the one I'm meant to spend my life with. I suppose time will tell.

For me, the beauty of Costa Rica was not just about being on a tropical vacation in a land far from home with surf, sand and sun. It was there that I found a much deeper connection: to myself, the land, the animals and the people. It is truly where I feel at home.

At times this book is a fun travel guide, at others a guide to a journey more spiritual in nature.

While my adventures took me deep into the jungle, where I contemplated the planet we live on and our place in it, they also took me down one way streets (the wrong way, mind you), with that "deer in the headlights" look as I tried to figure out how I turned into oncoming traffic and more importantly, how to get back on course.

There is much to know before you travel to a country like Costa Rica. My own experiences taught me that you won't necessarily find the information you need online or in the typical travel guides.

The stories of my adventures and life here on the Rich Coast are often comical and sometimes a tad scary and throughout the book, there is blend of fiction and nonfiction to keep you entertained and guessing, as to which is which. One small hint I will give you is that Troy isn't my love's real name. It is however another English name, much to my friends back home's chagrin. They really wanted my Latin Lover to come with a more traditional name.

I selected this photo for the introduction because of the coconut in it and what it represents. It's a green coconut, which means it's a young one. It can take an entire year for a coconut to develop into maturity and as we all know, good things come to those who are patient. However, I have since learned that the young green ones actually have more water in them, which is incredibly tasty and healthy for you as well.

So the coconut in this chapter represents me, in this young version, just beginning to reach out to life and spread my wings. I feel like my life really began when I turned thirty; it was then that I chose to let go of my past, move away from what had been my life for thirty years and start anew. And it was only a matter of time before I ended up traveling to Costa

Rica to further explore who I was and the person I wanted to be become.

It is my hope that you will see yourself in my journey and even if you choose to ignore my hard earned life lessons, at least pick up the travel tips I wish I'd had before I got to Costa Rica.

# Chapter 1

*Things to know before you go*

Until recently, Costa Rica was the only other Latin American country I had visited besides Mexico, but from what I can tell and what I've been told, it's one of the nicer countries to spend time in. However there are still some things you should know before you go. This list is definitely not all-inclusive but will give you a good idea of what to be aware of when visiting.

All of the insects you see in the States are way bigger in the tropical countries. I mean, way bigger. That little roach you saw at your favorite Chinese restaurant will be ten times larger (at least) in Costa Rica. They also have some insects you've probably never seen before and will never want to see again.

The only thing I really don't like having in my room are insects, especially the ones that fly. My rule is that the other animals in the room need to stay out of my personal space, or bubble, if you will. Twice however I have come into contact with a large lizard and an iguana. The two events scared both parties and made us both jump back away from one another. Fortunately, just opening a door will usually get any unwanted visitors out...you just have to be sure no new ones come in.

There was an unintentional massacre in my hotel room in La Fortuna. I noticed these somewhat large flying insects (by my standards, anything that comes in mass numbers and flies is large but they were about 1.5" long just to clarify) in my bathroom and occasionally a few would make their way into my room. So, I took my Burt's Bee's insect repellent (for the body, mind you) and sprayed it around the bathroom window. I left for two hours, went for a hike, and when I returned there were at least two hundred dead on the window, the bathtub, the ceiling, the walls, the floor, everywhere. It was awful and I felt even more guilt because my intention was only to keep them out of the room, not to draw them in and kill an entire colony!

*Close encounters of the amphibian kind*

The geckos are also all over the place, indoors and out. With every trip I've taken, there has been a chirping sound in my room, which I've never been able to distinguish. On my fourth visit, Troy told me that the geckos made this sound. Many times I thought there was a bird in my room because it was truly that loud.

There are also dart frogs of which I've only seen the orange/red and green/black varieties but I understand there are other color combinations. On the Caribbean side, these little guys were all over the place and they especially liked hanging outside the door of my bungalow. But they didn't seem to mind me and we reached an unstated agreement to leave each other alone. I saw the green/black frogs on the Pacific side on the Osa Peninsula and in Panamá. They got their name because the poison in the frog had been used by indigenous tribes in their weapons, which were, of course, darts.

*Scorpions (my astrological sign so I feel like I have a kinship with them)*

I have not yet seen a scorpion but have been told they exist in many parts of the country. While the scorpions in Costa Rica are not poisonous, they do still sting. As we were entering a coffee plantation, I asked my tour guide if there were scorpions living amongst the coffee fields. He answered, "Yes, while they're not poisonous, you'll have a very painful area where they stung you for about 24 hours". Delightful.

I visited a massage therapist on my first trip that was stung shortly after giving me a massage. She was stung on the hand as she pulled out new sheets from a dresser to put on the table. It seemed to cause her an excruciating amount of pain and I was glad I'd already received services, as she was unable to give any massages for the rest of the week we were there!

*Snakes*

While there are many kinds of snakes in Costa Rica, there are a few that are poisonous and can kill you or cause serious damage to your body.

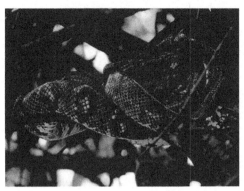

Unlike the boa constrictor pictured here which is not so easy to spot, the viper snake is small, bright yellow and deadly. It is with much sadness the only pictures I have are a little blurry, taken a few feet away from the snake while my sister looked on, horrified I was that close. It's not like it was moving; it was just taking a siesta on a tree trunk. I'm still hoping I'll find another one and get a better shot. I'm a little crazy when it comes to getting the shot.

Another poisonous snake is the fer-de-lance. I've encountered this one as well. I was in La Fortuna on the hanging bridges. I was by myself, enjoying a walk in the pouring rain on a bouncing metal bridge which was secured by treetops, when a man with a machete came up from behind me. My first thought was, Oh God, why is this man carrying a machete? Do I make a run for it? Of course, I was in my ked sandals on a bouncing metal bridge so running really was not an option. I'm also terrified of heights.

As it turned out, he was a nice man who worked at the bridges and he had killed the deadly snake, which I had passed along the trail at some point. He was carrying it on a stick (in the non-machete hand) and put it down on the ground so I could take a picture of it. Not realizing yet the snake was dead, and using my limited Spanish, I asked him "Muerta"? "Si, muerta", he replied. He got the snake all curled up for me so I could get a good shot and then picked it back up with the end of the stick and went along the path. He left the snake at the entrance and two men standing nearby told me, "Venenosa". "Sí, entendido", I replied.

Sadly, this wasn't my first run-in with a machete. During a trip through Mexico with an ex-boyfriend he pulled the Jeep over to the side of the road to ask a man, carrying a machete, if we were on the right road. Nothing happened, of course, but I do remember freaking out and yelling at him about his lack of concern for my safety. We also had a little incident with a bull on that trip, but that's another story.

*Domesticated Animals*

Speaking of which, the cows are different here in Costa Rica. I tried to explain it to friends at home and they just don't get it. Troy went into great detail when I brought it up to him but I didn't take notes, so I'll just stand by my claim that they are different.

Besides the wild animals, which hang out everywhere, Costa Rica also has lots of domesticated animals that hang out on the roads...without supervision from a farmer. Once, four horses were just taking a casual stroll down a road. Another time, it was a herd of goats. They seemed to know where they were going but it was still bizarre to see them running down the road without a shepherd in sight. About ten minutes after the herd had gone past, we heard one goat crying out and saw him running down the road. He was probably sidetracked by some grass and belatedly trying to catch up.

Also, there are always random dogs, chickens, cats and cows that walk along the road. You'll also see cowboys (called Caballeros or, if you're in certain regions, Sabaneros) herding their cows in the middle of principal roads as if they served no other purpose. Just be on the lookout and know that you may have to slow down for a cow in the road.

One thing I've noticed on each of my trips is there really isn't any road kill. I see dead animals on the road almost every day where I live in California. Troy and I only saw one bird in the road but given the amount of animals that are around, you would expect more. Apparently, with so few cars on the road the animals have time to cross the road without being hit. We saw numerous iguanas scurry across the road and once, a cool green lizard darted in front of us. When we saw the dead bird I got a sad look on my face and Troy, trying to be sweet, said to me, "He's sleeping".

*Mosquitoes*

It all depends on the time of year and location. I've had trips where I didn't get any bites and didn't use any repellent and then I've had trips where I lathered on the repellent and came home with huge welts up and down my legs. I've been told Costa Rica doesn't have a problem with malaria (rarely does a case show up) so pills aren't needed before you go. Of course, check with your local doctor or CDC for the most updated information. In this crazy, ever-changing world, you never know what's going to happen next.

The beaches also have a little insect called "no-see-ums". I didn't believe that was the name at first but that is truly what they call them. So much for those fantasies of hooking up with a guy on a tropical beach, portrayed in the movies. They are absolutely precluded by the reality of being bitten alive.

*Giant Orb Spiders*

Next to flying insects, spiders are probably my least favorite insect and when I found a picture of an orb that was larger than my hand in the location I visited on my fourth trip, I became a little concerned. Like I said, every insect you see in the States is muy grande in Costa Rica. The picture I saw was of a bird (yes, a bird) trapped in this huge orb's web. It makes my skin crawl just thinking about it. It took me seven trips to Central America but I finally did see two large orbs in Panamá. I wouldn't say they were giant but they were definitely bigger than your average spider.

You'll want to be careful on hikes to not run into spider webs. First, because you'll be destroying the home of another living being but secondly, walking into a spider web is never pleasant. Many years ago, I managed hundreds of acres of landscaping and, because webs can appear invisible in some lights, I would walk directly into them and feel the crinkling of the web on my hair and face. Trust me, it's not something you want to experience.

*Monkeys*

There are four types of monkeys that call Costa Rica home. They can be found in most of the jungle habitats and some of the tree-lined beaches. While they are very interesting, please remember these are wild animals. Do not give them food, or leave food out. Also, if one does come up to you, it is best not to touch them. Diseases can be spread (both ways) through contact. I also recommend that you abstain from using your flash while photographing animals for several reasons: it scares them, can temporarily damage their eyesight and they deserve to live a life without humans flashing bright lights at them.

Howler monkeys will almost never come down from their treetops. They are vegetarian and can get all of the food they need from the trees. They typically howl early in the morning and at sunset. If they get upset with you, the males will throw their feces at you. This happened to my brother-in-law on our first trip into the jungle. He wasn't actually doing anything to antagonize the male howler but we were a fairly large group of people and probably had disturbed the monkey's mid-day rest. Unfortunately for Mark, who was walking behind me, he got hit right in the face with the howler's feces. I'm still laughing about it today. However I was a good sister-in-law and offered him my antibacterial spray.

While howlers never come down from the trees, white faced monkeys do and they're fairly assertive about their needs and wants. This is where the whole "don't feed the animals" advice comes into play. White faced monkeys will come down and literally grab whatever is in your hand and take it away from you. They will also scavenge through your belongings if you leave them unattended.

Sadly, those are the only two monkeys I've had the chance to see in the natural jungle. I have had the opportunity to see endangered spider monkeys but that was at an animal sanctuary. I have yet to see the fourth type of monkey, the squirrel monkey, which is the smallest monkey in Costa Rica.

*Hotel Considerations*

With all of the restrictions on airline baggage, it's a good thing to ask your hotel if they have basic necessities so you don't have to drag them with you. Many hotels also prefer that you use their toiletries because they may have been specifically designed for the country's water systems (i.e. biodegradable soaps).

You'll also want to be prepared with the knowledge that you may not be able to flush your toilet paper. If there is a sign requesting that you not do this, please respect it. The sewer systems in Costa Rica are not the same as they are in the US and these hotels do clean out the trashcans at least once per day. It's not a pretty thing to think about but you need to be aware and respectful of this developing country. Not every hotel makes this request but depending on their location and the age of the hotel, you might come across one in your travels.

My first trip I stayed at a lovely retreat center on the Caribbean coast. I was traveling in a group and had brought an old college friend. She was horrified at the thought of putting the toilet paper into the trashcan and refused to do it. I was horrified at her complete disrespect for the retreat center and the rainforest in which we were staying. It should be noted she also refused to change the toilet paper roll when it was finished. Maybe she has some bathroom issues of which I was never aware.

*Cultural Considerations*

While Costa Rica does have one of the best educational systems, universal health care and many other positive aspects, including electing a woman in their 2010 presidential election, it is still developing in many ways. There is undoubtedly beauty and diversity but there is also poverty (or at least, poverty according to US standards). One should not think they are going to Maui (as I was told by the friend mentioned above on the last day of our trip and the last day we ever spoke) when they visit Costa Rica. Just because it's tropical and has beautiful beaches does not mean it has the same economy or way of life as the United States.

Another sensitivity, which I learned about from Troy, and confirmed with other Central and South Americans, was regarding the use of the word American to refer exclusively to things and people from the United States. Troy informed me that he didn't like it when people use the word in that context because he also lives in the Americas. I personally no longer use the term American to describe myself out of respect for his point that it's actually quite arrogant to think of people from the States as the only Americans. While I used to fill out the Nationality section of immigration forms with the term American, now I just write USA. You'll also find throughout this book that I have used the word US or States in lieu of America.

*The Costa Rican way of life (AKA Pura Vida)*

Much can be said about the motto of the Costa Rican culture: Pura Vida (translated: Pure Life). I've seen it taken to the extreme with negative consequences but I've also seen it as a way to live one's life to the fullest, enjoying every precious moment.

The mantra embodies the notion of living in the present moment. This is something I already strive for as a yoga teacher but find difficult to accomplish at times in the States. It's much easier for me to accept the present in Costa Rica.

I'm there to relax, play, have the time of my life; even the rockiest of roads are handled with skill and ease (at least most of the time). Pura Vida is about seeing the beauty that exists all around us and appreciating every breath we take in and exhale we give out.

I think I struggle more in the States because I get so caught up in my busy life between my job, commute, making time for friends and family, etc, I forget to just have fun and be grateful for the life I've been given. So often, my life is set on cruise control and I forget that life is meant to be lived to its fullest, each and every day.

I am so grateful for Troy, as he always reminds me to slow down, to not worry and to just be present. Life is always going to have its ups and downs but with a Pura Vida mindset, you'll find yourself living in a much healthier and more balanced manner. I think I lead a slower pace when I'm in Costa Rica but according to Troy, I'm still moving too quickly, so clearly I have room for improvement.

Some things to note about this different way of life: food service generally takes longer in Costa Rica. I'm not speaking about the multitude of fast food establishments, which have discouragingly popped up around the country, but the local restaurants. The server may be on a break when you arrive and s/he will get to you when they are ready. RELAX. You are no longer in the rat race of the States. Once in paradise, enjoy yourself and breathe in to this beautiful moment. Why are we always in such a hurry? Seriously, slow it down.

I do admit there are times when the slowness of the locals can be frustrating. Trying to book hotel reservations and determine availability prior to booking flights can be a daunting task. It can take days for some hotels to respond with the information you're looking for and by that time, the fare (or frequent flyer miles in my case) has increased and the whole trip has to be reassessed.

Short of calling the hotel and paying the exorbitant fees that AT&T charges (which I finally had to do), I remind myself that practicing patience is a lifelong endeavor...and it will all be worth it in the end. I highly recommend using services like Skype and Vonage so as to avoid paying those ridiculous international fees that regular phone companies charge.

Costa Ricans also don't like to say No. They think it's offensive. I've had firsthand experience with this and it wasn't until I read "The Golden Door to Retiring and Living in Costa Rica" that I finally understood why I had so many miscommunications with Troy. Instead of saying "No", he would say things like, "It's complicated", "I just don't know", "I will see", etc.

*Spanish/English*

Most hotels in Costa Rica have an English speaking staff. While their fluency may be limited, everyone I've ever met has tried very hard to learn English. They are also happy to help you with your Spanish. I studied French in high school and college so I need all the help I can get with this new linguistic challenge. I know most of the nouns (at least, the common ones) but learning how to conjugate the verbs has been my nemesis. I also find I try to translate what I'm saying into French first and then into Spanish. It can be very tiring and confusing but I believe it's only polite to try to speak the national language when traveling.

## The Rain and Other Weather Conditions

I love the rain in Central America. Troy likes to say the air feels "fresh" when it rains and I couldn't agree more. I never carry an umbrella, even in an outright downpour. Staff members at the hotels I've stayed in were always trying to hand me an umbrella but I love the feel of the rain on my skin, cleansing my body of all of the toxins I accumulated during the 330 or so days a year that I live in the States.

Blessedly, Costa Rica is not in the hurricane zone. That is one less thing for you to be concerned about when selecting travel dates. I did, however, have one trip where it felt like the skies were opening up and Mother Nature was releasing the largest tropical storm I had ever seen. There was a torrential downpour for four straight days in August 2007. I still went out sans umbrella. Though my camera is not waterproof, I've learned it can take a beating of rain and still work (do not try that at home, I'm a professional).

In general, the temperature will always be between 75 and 85°F. There will be times when it gets a little cooler if you're inland and if you're on the coast, it can get hotter. The nights generally cool down. Between December and April, the weather will be mild, very little rain (perhaps an afternoon thunderstorm) and there will be a lot less insects to contend with. This is their summer so expect to pay higher prices for lodging. May through November is considered the "green" season which is a nice way of saying you're going to get wet. However, unless you get caught in a really bad storm like the one I mentioned before, you'll most likely only experience a few days of rain and much of that will take place at night.

Don't let the rain stop you from enjoying your vacation. The weather is still warm and there is so much to see and do! If you're like me and don't want to carry an umbrella, just bring a lightweight plastic parka. It will keep the rain off and give you a place to store your camera.

*Sounds*

I wish I could insert the sounds of the rainforest into this book. Perhaps someday that technology will be readily available but for now, I will try my best to describe them. (And you can always pick up a nature CD that will create the sounds as well.)

Upon waking, there are the sounds of the howler monkeys and birds, perhaps a little rain hitting the canopy of the trees and the sounds of waves crashing if you're at the beach. The howlers start howling at 5:30 a.m. generally with the sunrise. You might also hear geckos chirping, cows, and even roosters depending on where you're staying. In Nicaragua, there was a rooster who woke me up, every morning at 3:30 a.m. He was on a neighboring island but the sound still carried across the water to my room.

There are over 850 bird species in Costa Rica, each with their own song. They, too, can be seen and heard throughout the day but the best time for viewing is in the early morning or as the sun is setting. They are out finding their food at this time; hence the adage, "the early bird gets the worm". Costa Rica is a place to which US birds migrate and I had the opportunity to view a Baltimore Oriole one sunny January morning in Santa Barbara de Heredia.

*Sunrise/Sunset*

Costa Rica doesn't participate in daylight savings time so the time change you experience will all be a matter of when you visit. For example, if you're traveling from the Pacific Time zone and you are traveling in April, the time difference will only be one hour (ahead). If you're traveling in January, the time change will be two hours ahead.

While the US, in its summer months, experiences daylight until 8:00 or 9:00 at night, in Costa Rica, the sun rises and sets at the same time year round: about 5:30 a.m. and 5:30 p.m.
I highly recommend getting up to watch the sunrise. I know, vacation is a time when you're supposed to sleep in but generally the mornings and early afternoon are the time to get out and enjoy the natural world since it may start raining in the late afternoon and into the evening.

There is also something special about watching the sunrise and acknowledging the start of a new day. Each day we have in our life we can make a difference so why waste it sleeping when we could be out doing something, learning something or helping someone.

*Roads, street signs and street names (or lack thereof)*

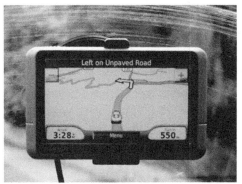

There are some great highways and roads in Costa Rica, however there are also many roads that need improvement. Driving in the city of San Jose is best left to the professionals or the GPS for the adventurous at heart.

As for street signs or street names, they don't have either. I'm not kidding. It is rare to see a street sign since they don't have names. For example, when I stayed at the Harmony Hotel in Nosara, the mailing address was 200 meters west of Hotel Café de Paris (another hotel which was just up the road and one I don't recommend). Add in the city and the region and you've got the mailing address - no number or street name needed.

Coincidentally, this is how I ended up going down a one-way road in Santa Barbara. The GPS told me to turn left in 250 meters but I'm not all that familiar with the metric system. (At the time, I didn't realize you could change the program in the GPS.) When I came to the stop light, I turned onto what I thought was a two way street. Let me be really clear. There was not a single sign that would indicate that the road was one-way only. The roads are so narrow in general that it didn't really surprise me to see such a small narrow street.

Then there are signs on the main highways that indicate potential problems ahead. They're written in Spanish though, which isn't much help if you don't speak the language. Sometimes you can deduce what they mean, even without a strong vocabulary. For example curvas peligrosas. You can presume that curvas is curves and so perhaps there are some curves ahead. However, ceja la pasa puzzled me until I tried to cross a one-lane bridge with oncoming traffic. I think I was supposed to wait until all of the traffic in the opposite direction had passed... My bad.

Troy (who I promise will be fully introduced later in the book) and I met a woman at breakfast one morning in Manuel Antonio who was incredibly surprised that I had rented a car. While I agree that some roads can be scary, it's part of the adventure. It's also such a pain to have to wait for taxis or shuttles. I'd rather be able to get in the car and go. As a photographer, I also want to be able to stop the car whenever I want and that's hard to do with public transportation or a hired shuttle.

There is also a lack of streetlights in Costa Rica. The main cities have them but most of the rural areas do not. When possible, it's a good idea to plan ahead and be at your location before dark.

The speed limit is also much slower than what you're probably accustomed to in the States. Even on some open roads, the maximum speed allowed is only 80 KPH which is about 48 MPH. Most roads will be between 40 and 60 KPH (24 to 36 MPH). While you may not see many cops, they are out there with their radar guns. I have, however, seen a vehicle pass a police officer on the left (on the oncoming traffic side) and the officer didn't pursue him. I'm not suggesting you try it but I have seen it done by the locals.

*Cell phones*

With the exception of one spot in Manuel Antonio and while staying at Lapa Rios on the Osa Peninsula (which purposefully doesn't have any cell phone towers), I've really never had a problem with being able to use either my cell phone or the one I rent through the car rental agency (which I recommend doing). This surprises me because even in certain cities along the coast where I live in California, I'm unable to get cell phone service. How is it that I can get cell service in remote locales in a developing country but not in the developed country of my birth? I don't know if it's illegal to text or call people while driving but I wouldn't recommend it. Driving in Costa Rica is hard enough without having the distraction of a cell phone.

*Local Eateries*

I encourage you to avoid the typical US fare you'll see in many of the cities and support the local restaurateurs. Costa Rica has what is called a "soda" which is similar to a small café where you can purchase light food and drinks. Alongside the roads, you will often come across fruit and vegetable stands which are produced by the local farmers. Supporting these establishments enables you to give back to the local community and reduces your footprint while traveling. Plus, eating a sweet, juicy mango or pineapple that was just freshly picked is pure bliss. I promise!

## Chapter 2

*EcoTourism*

When I travel, I seek out lodging that has sustainable, "green" practices in place. An enormous amount of waste goes into tourism and at this point in my life it's appalling to me to think about traveling to a foreign country and adding to their environmental problems. Personally, I always carry my reusable stainless steel water bottle when I travel and I now bring the canvas bag my nephew sent me one Christmas. Then, when I go to the market, I don't have to take one of their plastic, pink and white striped bags.

I do rent SUV's when I'm there, however I do so because of the conditions of the roads. The choice to rent a SUV serves to provide some security in the knowledge that I'm less likely to break down in the middle of nowhere, caught in a flash flood or stuck in the mud. Therefore, choosing to transport myself via SUV is a conscious contribution to my safety that I cannot set aside, particularly when I'm traveling on my own.

Traveling in a sustainable way does seem to make the trip a little more expensive but I believe that it is worth it. I'm also very passionate about sharing the information that I have learned about being a compassionate consumer, concerned with taking care of our planet.

In the United States, we generally don't pay the external costs of the products we purchase every day such as food, gas and other retail items. Many of us have never even heard of the term, which simply means paying the unshielded price for the items we purchase every day. Firstly, the government subsidizes our food and gas so it is less expensive from a purely monetary standpoint. Secondly, we are also usually unaware of the cost to the environment and local community. For example, if we were to pay the real cost of gas for our cars, the price per gallon would be two to four times higher per gallon as we'd be paying to offset the pollution we're causing. This much more expensive reality would make many of us think twice about the types of vehicles we drive and the amount of driving we do.

By choosing to stay at Eco Lodges, you are helping to offset the external costs of your trip. Eco Lodges take into account the triple bottom line: People, Planet and Profit. These employers consider the people who work at the hotel as well as the local community, offering staff members a living wage as well as training and advancement. EcoLodges are also good stewards of the planet; reducing their ecological footprint and educating others, both visitors and staff, to do the same.

At the same time, a lot of "greenwashing" takes place these days. Hotels can say they are green but only do the bare minimum such as installing a low flow toilet or offering a bedding or towel change policy. When looking for a truly environmentally friendly hotel, you should check that most, if not all, of these practices in place:

- Environmentally friendly cleaning products.
- Reusable dispensers for shampoo, conditioner and soap.
- Non-chlorine products in pools.
- No pesticides or herbicides in gardens.
- Growing their own food and/or buying from local farmers.
- Designing their menus around local culture and seasonal food.
- Composting.
- Water filtration so the water from the taps is safe to drink.
- Recycling: not just in the common areas but in the guest rooms as well.
- Policies on towel and bedding changes.
- Hiring people from the local area to help support the local economy and the people in their community.
- Supporting the local community through projects (such as starting a recycling program or supporting a local school).
- They should be a part of a green certification program and/or working with other local hotels to initiate industry change.
  New buildings/structures are constructed wisely and with green materials.

Just like hotels, any tour company can claim that they are green. Here are a few tips to distinguish which ones are truly taking part in sustainable measures:

- The tour should be in small groups so as to lessen the impact on the environment and wildlife.
- Animals should be in the wild and never held captive unless at a rescue sanctuary or rehabilitation center.
- Your Guide should be experienced. They should understand how to make less of an impact, instructing visitors that they are entering someone's "home" and to speak softly when visiting natural places where wildlife may be mating, nesting, or just living. They should also not veer off the path, touch any animals or take anything from the environment.

As a traveler, you also have a responsibility in being a good steward. Every choice you make will make a difference, even if it seems small:

- Pick up trash when you see it
- Do not leave anything behind
- Ask questions
- When photographing, do not use the flash on animals
- Do not feed the animals or leave any food out.
- Be respectful and stay a safe distance away from wildlife (for both you and the animal).
- Never touch a wild animal or remove it from its home.
- Always be respectful and ask if it's okay to photograph people before taking their picture.
- If snorkeling or diving, take care to avoid touching coral, fish or marine animals like seals and dolphins, with any

part of your body – remember, they are living organisms just like you and me.
- Do not purchase animals or products made from animals.
- Do not purchase wood products made from unsustainable wood sources (look for FSC certified labels).
- Offset your travel with carbon credits.
- Dress to blend in.
- Act as an example to other tourists.
- Be aware and respectful of natural resources – water, electricity, etc.
- Stay in a town in which walking is a viable transportation option.
- Choose to support locally owned businesses, restaurants and artisans; not chains.
- Bring your own reusable water bottle and if you're going to be drinking coffee on the road, bring a reusable coffee mug.

One of my favorite quotes can be found in gift shops throughout Costa Rica on stickers and other merchandise:

*"If nothing changes soon will come the day, when we tell our children and the children of our children how beautiful this planet was once, and the animals that once inhabited it. You know what you have to do."*
Author Unknown

From the micro to the macro, we are all One and connected through this fragile web of life. With conscious choices, we can protect our precious planet and create a better world for all who live here. You will find additional resources and information at the end of this book.

## Chapter 3

*Samasati Yoga Retreat*
*Puerto Viejo*

March 2006

I had the opportunity to spend a week in paradise with the sun shining, two yoga classes a day, healthy and incredible tasting foods and adventures in the jungle and beaches as part of a yoga retreat. We were staying at Samasati, a retreat center and nature reserve in Puerto Viejo which had received "Four Leaves" from the Certification of Sustainable Tourism organization, a group based in Costa Rica. My sister had arranged the trip and I was very pleased with her choice to stay at a sustainable retreat center.

Unfortunately, my trip to paradise resulted in the loss of one of my best friends from college, though not physically. There were a few moments where I hoped that she would just disappear or at least take an earlier flight home. I really wish that before the trip she had taken the time to understand what she was getting herself into, but she found the reality of Costa Rica untenable.

I loved the bungalow we were staying in. She hated it, relentlessly talking about the quality of the construction and design, particularly her unhappiness that the windows did not contain glass, merely screens. As if these inconveniences weren't enough, there were lizards in the room. How could she possibly enjoy such a trip. On the other hand, we had hot water and electricity (most of the time), two beds, full sized bathroom, loft area and a hammock on a large deck in the middle of a rainforest. I found our accommodations to be everything that I could wish for in a developing country. If only our difference in perspective had been limited to our accommodations, we might have been able to salvage our friendship.

Puerto Viejo is the closest town to the retreat center and it has a great Caribbean feel to it. I had the opportunity to discover what chocolate looks like on the tree (it's a white or pink fruit, by the way) in a botanical garden and walked into town for lunch, shopping and to find an internet café. There were cats and dogs lounging in public spaces, children playing in the street and the people were friendly and helpful. If I could pick up the town and move it West, I'd move there in an instant. There are some good towns on the Pacific side but Puerto Viejo has a vibe that I just haven't found elsewhere. There were no fast food establishments and a lot less tourism than what I would find later in my travels.

We also went snorkeling and took a hike through the jungle, alongside a beach. I wasn't all that interested in the snorkeling part of the tour. It was my first experience and I found that wearing the mask and mouthpiece underwater brought on an overwhelming feeling of claustrophobia. Also, I felt incredibly challenged while wearing the fins; they dragged me down and I was terrified of touching any of the coral. I chose to end my snorkeling experience early and caught a few rays of sunshine on the boat, while watching the others in the water.

Our guide then drove the boat to the tip of Cahuita National Park. Unfortunately, as I was departing, I fell off the boat and into the water. People around me were panicking but I just laughed. I was wet and my backpack was wet but my camera was dry and that was what was most important to me at the time. As we sat and ate our lunches on this beautiful, calm, white sand beach, one of the white faced monkeys jumped down from the trees overhead and grabbed my friend's apple. It's probably another thing she's still mad at me about, especially since I thought it was pretty funny. That was also the day we saw the viper and if I remember correctly, she stayed pretty far away, probably furious, again, that I had taken her to some place with crazy cold-blooded, poisonous creatures. First her apple, then a poisonous snake to threaten her person... was nothing sacred? It was clear that she thought both Costa Rica and my loyalty left something to be desired.

The final straw was probably the lack of enjoyment she received from our zip line adventure, not that anyone forced her to do it, but she was pretty upset as we careened across the rainforest canopy to eighteen different platforms. Though perhaps it was the morning wakeup calls provided by the local howler monkeys. Either that or the rain, in the rainforest. Though we rarely had to deal with it, the drizzle while we were on the zip line did not thrill her like it did me. The construction of our bungalow was indeed built properly as none of the rain entered our living space, though she was not in the mood to look at that as an upshot.

This was my first visit to the Rich Coast and overall, I just loved it. It was at a time in my life when I was just beginning to learn about the environment and our place in it and this trip really opened my eyes to the beauty that exists on our planet and the need for a better understanding of why conservation is so very important, not just here in Costa Rica but in each of our daily lives because every action we take really does create a reaction for someone or something else, somewhere in the world.

## Chapter 4

*Nosara, Playa Guiones*

August 2007

I always knew I'd be back. It felt like home when I was there and with such a profound connection, it was only a matter of time before I found a way to return to the Rich Coast.

My opportunity materialized when I started working for a nonprofit whose founder did international speaking engagements and one of them happened to be in Costa Rica. As a nonprofit organization there wasn't any money to pay for my trip, but I didn't care!

I was going back to Costa Rica and this time to the Pacific Coast: Playa Guiones, Nosara, Guanacaste on the Nicoya Peninsula to be exact.

The travel arrangements were being organized through a "yoga adventure" company. Their promotional materials made the accommodations sound lovely and well, accommodating. The theme of the all female retreat was empowering women to be their true selves.

When we arrived at the hotel, we could barely get the receptionist to acknowledge us, much less give us the keys to our room. I learned later that no one from the yoga adventure company or any of the retreat leaders had ever been to this hotel. Our room was a total dive with gigantic insects crawling all around. The beds didn't even come with blankets. Like I mentioned previously, it does actually get cold at night. On our second day, I went to the front desk to ask if we could get a few blankets for the room but was told that housekeeping didn't work on Sunday's and we'd have to wait until they returned on Monday.

After we settled into the room, the woman I was traveling with and my boss decided that it would be nice to go for a walk on the beach. As we're walking out of the hotel, we run into the three leaders of the retreat and stop to chat. The conversation left me with little hope that the retreat activities were going to compensate for the unsatisfactory conditions and service in the hotel.

The main leader, we'll call her Anne, was telling us how they had just gotten back from visiting a community, which was being developed alongside the beach in Nosara. The land was owned by a man who had a popular retreat center in the States and she mentioned that the purchase of the homes was "By invitation only". Whoa. Wait, what? Really? This world renowned yogi was participating in a community that not only excludes local citizens from owning property there (in their own country) but is also destroying the natural landscape of the area?

I thought to myself, "Okay, suck it up, Chrissy. So, she's not all you imagined she'd be. You know, a yogi who lives by yogic principles and who believes in oneness and inclusivity over exclusivity." Still, I couldn't help but be disappointed and a tad angry. The people purchasing these properties weren't even residents, much less citizens, of this beautiful country. The land in the area had to be somewhat devastated in order to build on it as I doubt it was just a dirt lot begging to have US style homes built on it.

I didn't really think things could get worse and I tried to put it behind me. The events that followed continued the downward spiral and left me with a sinking fear that no amount of optimism was going to be able to redeem this experience. First, the three leaders (not my boss) were extremely late to dinner and they didn't sit at the community tables but instead sought out a table for themselves. They were also staying at a house in a private location so no one really knew where they were when they weren't in the yoga studio teaching or giving an evening program. Almost every meal that followed, they either showed up late or not at all. Lunches found them down at the Harmony Hotel; probably because the food was much better than the hotel where the retreatants were staying.

When I saw the theme of the evening program, Empowering Women, I thought the topic sounded like great thing to talk about. It's certainly needed in today's society. I envisioned discussions about ways to become more assertive and empowered in our daily lives, both personally and professionally. I couldn't help but wonder why the reality included an awful lot of male bashing. The yin and the yang teach us we need a balance of both male and female energy in order to provide a healthy and stable life for ourselves and our planet. The male bashing was followed by goddess and priestess work; including calling to our spirit guides, to women who have passed on, and bringing them into the room to join us in dance and song. This was way too esoteric for me. I may live in Sonoma County and teach yoga but that doesn't mean I dance under the full moon naked (not that it was a part of the program, as far as I know. Although I did hear a few of the women went skinny dipping one night!).

With such deep work going on, it was even more disappointing to see the lack of support that was given by the group leaders to the participants. They actually had the brilliant idea to break everyone into small groups and if a problem arose (such as a mental or emotional crisis, which happened a lot on this retreat), it was the group who was responsible to care for the person, not the trained leaders because they were never around.

By day 3, I'd had enough. I packed up my suitcase and took the last available room at the Harmony Hotel hoping that the name was a good omen, especially since it matched up with my business name and the name of my cat.

The first hotel was so awful that several of the other participants had already left the hotel and relocated to the Harmony but were still participating in the retreat. Personally, I had thrown in the towel on the entire week and was going to spend what was left of my vacation in the warm morning sunshine and torrential afternoon rainstorms.

One of the girls participating in the retreat, Jodie, was actually living in Nosara and had a 4Runner so she offered me a ride to the Harmony Hotel. I was grateful for the kind gesture as it was pouring rain and I would have had to drag my suitcase down a dirt road. Of course, I would have done anything to get out of that hotel and the retreat but was grateful for the alternative.

As I settled into my lovely room which had a king sized bed (with a down comforter, mind you), wardrobe closet, beautiful bathroom and large private patio with an outdoor shower, I considered the events that had taken place over the last few days and was relieved I was strong enough, no, empowered enough, to take control of my life and leave a bad situation. I took a long hot shower and refreshed, ventured out to the hotel lobby to see what there was to do.

It was then that I met Troy. He was a cutie, to be sure. He spoke very good English, had an amazing smile, and a beautiful body, not that I was checking him out or anything... much. I asked if I could use the internet and he told me to come around through the back door of the reception area to use a computer there.

We made a little small talk and he asked me if I liked to go out to eat and go dancing. I said sure, dancing was always fun, food was good. I didn't really understand at the time that he was asking me out. Then he asked me again and was more clear, "Do you want to go out tomorrow night?" "Oh, okay. Yeah. That sounds fun", I answered. He inquired, "You don't have to go back to your yoga retreat?" "Nope", I responded with a mischievous smile. A date was set. Now my only thought was…what was I going to wear? I hadn't really brought date clothes on the yoga retreat.

I wrote a quick email to my best friend Mike to tell him the story of the last few days, anticipating the sound of his laugh at the news. He wouldn't be surprised to read that I was in a foreign country, pretty much on my own and was going out on a date. He knew that I could take care of myself and he didn't need to worry, just sit back and enjoy life vicariously through me.

The next morning, I went for a walk on the beach as there were just a few moments of sunshine before the rain started again. The warm winter sun and the humid air felt so good on my skin.

I walked onto the tide pools (being careful where I stepped) and watched as a crab hung onto the edge of a large rock as a large wave crashed over him. I was so intrigued by this. So often as a yoga teacher I'm asking my students to "let go". However, I think there are also times when you just have to hang on like this crab was doing; to hold on to what you believe in, and know everything will be okay.

While the warm sun felt good on my skin, I had forgotten to put on sunscreen and my shoulders were burned to a crisp. That afternoon, Troy saw me, touched my shoulder and said, "Caliente!" I could only laugh, there was nothing I could do but buy a bottle of aloe lotion from the gift shop and hope it didn't peel while I was still in Nosara.

After he was done with work for the day, Troy came to my room to pick me up and told me we'd be going to dinner at La Luna which is a restaurant and bar on Playa Pelada, just north of Nosara. His friend, Claudia, worked there and would give us a ride. She had a truck (with a manual transmission, mind you) and I remember being so impressed with her driving skills. There was another torrential rainstorm that night and she was driving on dirt roads, up and down hills, with incredible ease. It was only a 2-seater truck so Troy sat in the truck bed with an umbrella, ever the gentleman. When we stopped at her friend's house, Troy opened up the passenger side door and leaned in to give me our first kiss. He was still holding the umbrella to keep the water from getting inside the vehicle. It was such a cute gesture and still brings a smile to my face.

During the drive, Claudia and I spoke about the extensive construction I was seeing in town. She said that while it had its good points, such as improving the local economy with US money, it was also destroying the environment and local communities. She hoped that the government and local communities would be able to find a balance between new construction and conservation. I don't know too many people in the States who look at a new condominium development and consider the impact it has on the environment. Our discussion definitely gave me some things to consider.

When we arrived at La Luna, Troy explained to me the different national beers (Bavaria, Pilsen and Imperial) and we ordered a round to drink before dinner. While our meals were being prepared, Troy took my hand and led me outside for a walk on the beach. It had stopped raining, for the moment, and the full moon was peeking out from the clouds, radiating onto the sand and water. I loved the feel of Troy's hand in mine as we walked along the beach; it just felt so natural and fit into mine so well.

We ordered a plate of tapas to share and hung out at the bar making small talk while watching a very drunk man from the States try to roll a joint unsuccessfully. Later, we ordered a few more beers and sat on one of the couches at the restaurant just getting to know one another, listening to the music playing in the bar.

When we arrived back at the hotel, we decided to take a walk down to the beach. Troy had a flashlight with him and would point out the puddles so I wouldn't walk into them (he didn't yet know that I'm the kind of girl who likes to splash in puddles; always a kid at heart). When we got to the beach, we found a piece of driftwood and sat down on it. In between kisses, we watched the lightning strike out on the ocean and listened to the thunder overhead. His kisses were mesmerizing...making me forget I was being eaten alive by no-see-ums. When the storm headed our way, we ran under an open-air palapa for cover and we continued making out while the rain poured down around us.

That night, and those that followed, left such a sweetness in my body, mind and spirit – more than anything I could have ever felt or learned on the retreat, had I stayed. It had been a very long time since I let my heart open up that way...almost seven years to be exact. While I had dated over the past seven years, there was something different when I was with Troy. It might have been easier since I knew it couldn't go anywhere but somehow, Troy took down the wall around my heart that I had built so many years earlier.

Troy had to work for the remainder of my holiday in Nosara but we were able to spend a little more time together over the next few days. He often worked the night shift, until 10, so I would leave my door unlocked and he would let himself in. I can still remember exactly how his body felt sleeping next to me; how warm he was and the touch of his skin next to mine. Of course, he snored...so while I didn't get much sleep, it is still a sweet memory.

## Chapter 5

*Playa Tamarindo*

January 2008

When I returned home from Nosara, I found myself feeling both elated and sad. While it was likely that Troy flirted with all of the single girls traveling through the hotel, the intense connection we had shared made me wonder if there was something more there. I contacted the hotel only four days after I had left, to see if we could stay in touch only to find out he was no longer employed there.

I couldn't help but wonder if the hotel management team had found out about us and terminated his employment, as comingling with the guests was a big no-no. I asked the hotel if they could put me in touch with him and they gave me his cell phone number. I tried to call him a few times that month but it always went straight to voicemail. I eventually gave up and went back to my daily life.

A few months later, sitting in my car, waiting for a yoga class to start my thoughts wandered the warmth of Costa Rica and the love I had left behind. I reached for my cell phone and dialed Troy's number. It rang. I couldn't believe it! A sexy voice on the other end of the phone answered, "Diga" (slang for "hi" in Spanish). I wasn't sure what to say...would he remember me? "Troy?" "Si", he answered. I told him it was Christina from Harmony (he always called me Christina). "Ahhhhh, Christina, como estas!"

We talked for an hour that night. I learned after the fact I didn't have an international calling plan but it didn't matter. I had reconnected with Troy! He still had that sweet, sexy way of making my skin tingle, even from 3,000 miles away. He was living in La Fortuna, near Arenal volcano, closer to his hometown. He had left the Harmony Hotel by choice the same weekend I went home. Only the undercurrent of excitement I felt at reconnecting, finally, overshadowed my relief.

As the end of graduate school drew near, I decided I wanted to celebrate by making another trip to the Rich Coast. I told Troy of my plans and we decided we would meet at the beach and then go inland to La Fortuna where he would show me around. I was so excited to see my love again and to make a third trip to this beautiful country!

Over the next five months, Troy and I spoke almost every day. We laughed so much and I couldn't wait to see him and feel his tender kisses and warm body next to mine again.
By May we had become so close and the intensity was almost too much to bear. Troy arranged for a rental car for me through a friend's company and we made plans to meet in

Playa Tamarindo (which he calls "Tamagringo" since there are so many people from the US living there). He would be taking a few days off from work to play with me at the beach and neither of us could wait.

May 2008

May finally arrived. School was done and I was free from all responsibilities for nine days. Stepping off the plane, I walked down the stairs to the tarmac in the absence of a terminal since Liberia is such a small airport. I inhaled deeply, relishing the humidity and warmth, which is Costa Rica. Birds flew around the open-air terminal as I passed through immigration and waited for my bags. Luggage in hand, I made my way outside the terminal, only to be bombarded by taxi drivers but not a single had a sign with my name on it to indicate that they were waiting for me specifically.

I reached for my cell phone only to realize I don't know how to make a call on it from an international location. As I tried to figure it out, drivers wanting me to take their taxi constantly approached me. I did not feel totally safe and I was more than a little disappointed that the rental car company forgotten about me. I tried not to panic but could definitely feel it creeping up on me.

The rental company didn't show and I tentatively allowed a driver to arrange for a female taxi driver to take me to the agency. I was anxious to get my trip started. I took a deep breath and tried to reassure myself that everything would be okay.

At the agency I was issued a Nissan Almera (which kind of looks like a Sentra). It wasn't exactly my idea of the perfect car for the conditions of the road in Costa Rica but I decided it would do. I also came to find out the insurance for the car was almost the same price as the daily rental rate. I didn't want to take any chances with theft or damage so I took every option available. I also rented a cell phone so that Troy and I could talk without huge international fees. The clerk gave me a map and told me to follow the signs to Playa Tamarindo, telling me at one point I'll need to look for a gas station and make a right as there may not be a sign. He assured me that since gas stations are few and far between in Costa Rica, it will be easy to determine the correct place to turn.

Once in town, I couldn't seem to find my directions to the hotel and I ended up on a very rough dirt road heading away from the town center. I pulled over to call the hotel for assistance. I'm told that I am on the correct road and to follow it until I see the hotel. Neither the Almera nor my driving experience was accustomed to that sort of road conditions. I worried that I would pop a tire but had no choice but to take a deep breath and drive as slowly as possible.

Fortunately, Hotel Capitan Suizo wasn't too much farther down and a friendly staff member greeted me. Welcome drink ticket in hand, I followed a bellboy to Bungalow #2. Thankfully, after the start my vacation had, I loved the room. It was a split level with a canopy king size bed on the upper level and a futon couch with two additional chairs on the lower level. The bathroom was huge and even had a Jacuzzi tub. Top it all off with an outdoor shower and two separate places to sit and relax outside, just steps from the beach and I was beyond excited.

I immediately called Troy who asked, "Where have you been? I've been worried!" He laughed and said he was glad I was okay after I relayed the day's events. We confirmed his plan to get into town the following afternoon and then I settled into my hotel room, took a shower and then went to the restaurant for an early dinner. I was joined for dinner by one of the hotel cats sitting on the chair across from me.

I followed the sparkling lights of the fireflies as I walked back to my room. I hadn't seen fireflies since spending childhood summers in Short Hills, New Jersey with my mom's sister and her family. I remember we used to try to catch them in jars to watch them light up. As an adult, I'm quite content to just let them fly in front of me freely, leading me through the darkness.

Flipping through the hotel activity book, I saw an offering of Mayan Astrology readings. Interested, I called the front desk to book an appointment for the next day, just before Troy was to arrive.

The next morning I took a walk to Playa Langosta and was caught in a quick rainstorm. My hair and clothes were both still a little wet upon my return (although in the heat, everything dries pretty quickly) but I hardly noticed because a staff member in the lobby was holding a baby monkey named Sophie. I'd never seen a monkey this close and with camera in hand, I asked the woman if I could take a photo of the two of them. Shaking her head she walked toward me, gesturing that she would let me hold the monkey and take a photo of the two of us instead. Sophie fell immediately into my arms and crawled up to my shoulder. She played with my hair and nuzzled her head against mine.

When it came time to give her back to her caretaker, Sophie wouldn't let go. Her tail, which had been loosely wrapped around my neck, started to grasp tighter as a second caretaker came over to help. Sophie still wouldn't let go. Her little hands were clutching my hair and she started to cry out with discontent. I started to worry about my ability to breathe if she wrapped her tail any tighter. I now understand how strong a monkey's tail must be in order to swing from the trees and hang from branches! Eventually, the two caretakers dislodged her and Sophie showed us her angst by peeing all over the floor. While I wouldn't be charmed by this action in a human, I found it pretty amusing from Sophie. Fortunately, her caretaker ran her over to a tree and Sophie jumped onto a nearby branch.

The hotel had taken in Sophie along with a second monkey, Alice, because they were orphaned and injured. A local veterinarian had to amputate Alice's tail. Occasionally, monkeys are brought to the hotel by concerned local citizens who find them, in need of assistance. The hotel provides them with veterinary care and a safe place to grow and develop. The monkeys are free to live in the trees and can leave the hotel premises if they so desired. The hotel's ultimate goal for the monkeys is for them to be adopted by a local howler troop and to create families of their own. Since my visit, they have stopped letting guests interact with them directly, so I consider myself blessed.

I cherish the memory of my moments with Sophie as I learned so much from her. To feel her safely surrender into my arms and climb onto my shoulder to rest, silently placing her head against mine reminded me that there was no difference between her and I. While we may be of different species, we still want the same things: to be loved, held and cherished by another and to be kept safe from harm. In that moment, my perspective of life was illuminated with joy and truth but at the same time sorrow at the often times harsh reality. The howler monkey population in Costa Rica is declining because of development and deforestation. Uninsulated electrical lines also pose mortal danger to the monkeys as when they swing from the trees on to an uninsulated line they are electrocuted. Many of them fall to their death and those that live are severely burned.

At the time, I was just starting out in the field of conservation photography and meeting Sophie prompted me to create a photography book on the concept of oneness and living intentionally. So often, our lives remain on "auto-pilot" and we do not take into consideration the impact of our thoughts, words and actions on others, both locally and globally. As humans, we are able to change and to create a better world; each choice we make in our daily life can make a difference. I want people to understand that when we begin to recognize all that exists as an extension of the self, we will then act intentionally and peace, love and joy will flow outwards to all. I selected a howler monkey rescue and rehabilitation organization in Nosara, Costa Rica as one of the recipients of the net profits from my book. It is my hope people will read the book and be inspired to learn more about issues that concern them and to take action steps to create a kinder, safer, more beautiful world.

My day of making new friends continued as I met Nati for my Mayan Astrology reading later that morning. Nati and I have since become dear friends and I truly value her friendship. We are very much alike and I am so fortunate our paths have crossed. Nati proceeded to tell me in my reading that I was born on the day of the monkey, adding even more value to my encounter with Sophie. Nati told me that after turning 35, my life would change dramatically. She assured me that I could look forward to that being a time in my life when I truly step in to who I am and what I'm here on the planet to do. I asked about Troy as well and after assessing his date of birth she informed me that while we may have some complications, he is sincere and will love me.

During the reading, Troy called to tell me that he was stuck in Liberia as there was not another bus going to Tamarindo that afternoon. He asked if I could I come pick him up. While I really wanted to see him I didn't really want to make the hour drive back to Liberia, especially since it was getting dark. It was also raining and not showing any signs of stopping. In the background Nati arranged for her friend, who drove a taxi, to pick Troy up in Liberia. Troy was baffled as to how could I make arrangements so quickly but I thought it explained everything when I mentioned that a friend had taken care of it. Since Troy knew that I had only been in the country less than 24 hours and had shown up not knowing anyone, he was further confused as to how I had made a friend so quickly but I've always made friends and connected with people very easily. It's a gift.

With Troy now on his way, I went back to the room to get ready. I was so excited; my was heart racing, palms sweating and butterflies the size of a beautiful blue morpho were dancing around in my stomach. Time flew as I prepared for the reunion of "Christina" and Troy.

I put on my sexy new halter dress, which showed off my assets and hid my imperfections in a way that let me just feel comfortable in my own beauty. I was exceptionally pleased to have intentionally packed clothing appropriate for a date since I'd had a lack of them on hand the last time Troy and I had been together.

As I waited, I noticed cats and a family of raccoons eating the food the hotel provided for its resident felines. I watched the dynamic between the cats and the raccoons with great amusement because the raccoons were actually quite timid, waiting for the cats to take a break before they'd try to sneak a bite.

At long last, a taxi van pulled up delivering Troy. I had a huge smile on my face as we ran towards each other. He wrapped me in his arms squeezing tightly, giving me a kiss and said hello in a tone that sent shivers down my spine. The butterflies were gone leaving me to feel like a sixteen year old, hand in hand with her first love. Despite the initial rush, our companionability is more like that of two old lovers meeting after a long separation. When he kissed me it felt so natural to have his strong arms wrapped around me again.

Later that night we sat outside the bungalow on our private patio and listened to Bob Marley. We talked as he held my hand so gently, every once in awhile reaching over to kiss me sweetly. Once again I was eaten alive by mosquitoes, which, like the no-see-ums in Nosara, developed into huge red welts on the lower half of my legs. I didn't care a drop…I was with my love. Each morning as we woke, Troy would whisper to me with his sexy accent, "Buenos días, mi amor" and I'd smile and say it back as he kissed me and pulled me closer.

We spent the next few days walking around town, playing in the ocean, watching the incredible sunsets over the Pacific and making love. It was nothing shot of bliss.

Unfortunately, as we were leaving for Fortuna, some of the rosy sunshine of the situation began to dim. Troy had left a ripped piece of paper on the bathroom counter with another girl's contact information at a university in the states. I didn't relish finding that when I was supposed to be on this blissful holiday with my love. It wasn't that I naively believed that I was the only girl he would ever be interested in, just that it was a rude awakening from the cocoon of instant companionship we'd been enjoying. I confess that while I don't feel old in spirit, I definitely do not wish to compete with a twenty year college girl. I never confronted Troy about the piece of paper, since I could hardly make a claim to exclusivity but it was still a disappointment to find.

To further complicate matters, Troy got a call from his friend who wanted to come stay with him in La Fortuna. Troy asked if we could pick him up in Cañas and take him with us. I didn't anticipate that it would change our plans, so I agreed. I could not have been more mistaken. Troy was no longer going to stay with me at the hotel and when we did arrive in Fortuna several hours later, I had the sinking feeling I wouldn't see him again.

I contacted my dear friend Mike for moral support and his advice was for me to just go with the flow. Sometimes, I find the difference in male and female perspectives about a situation really comical, but I was not as amused in that moment. His assessment was that there wasn't anything I could do about any of it and I just needed to enjoy my time there. After all, wasn't I in paradise?

# Chapter 6

*Fortuna*

When it became apparent that Troy was not going to stay with me, I decided I'd find other lodging as I was not a fan of the hotel he had recommended in La Fortuna. When I travel alone, I like to stay at higher end hotels because they usually offer security and have a restaurant on the premises so I don't have to go out at night if I don't feel comfortable doing so.

I relocated the next morning but not before I locked the car keys in the trunk of the rental car. I started to wonder if perhaps I was on a hidden camera show, making fun of international tourists. I had to call the rental car agency for a spare set of keys, since there is no AAA available in Costa Rica, which resulted in about a three-hour drive for one of their employees. Once I had the ability to command my vehicle once more, I relocated to Hotel Los Lagos, which was located just outside of town but offered an incredible view of Arenal volcano.

The hotel also had crocodiles on the grounds which they said they were rehabilitating until their eventual released, however I'm not certain that they weren't there more for entertainment purposes. Hindsight is always 20/20.

One thing I loved about the hotel was their gardens. They were breathtaking and I took most of my flower photographs from the trip there. Since it was the beginning of May and the start of the wet season, I was really fortunate to see so many beautiful flowers in bloom.

While I was devastated at Troy's actions, I chose to make the most of my time in La Fortuna. Mike was right; I was in paradise. I spent a day at Tabacon Hot Springs and had one of the best casados ever made. Though the server didn't understand my request for a vegetarian version the first time, we were able to sort it out.

Tabacon is a little pricey and I'm sure there are other hot springs in the area that you can visit that are less expensive but Tabacon is world renowned and I wanted to see if it lived up to its reputation. In addition to the incredible lunch, I have to say the springs truly are an experience not to be missed. The pools are so refreshing and relaxing; it's like getting a hot stone massage but better because of the beautiful environment that surrounds you.

After my day at the Hot Springs, I visited Arenal Observatory later that afternoon. From what I could tell, this was one of the best places to actually see the active side of the volcano. There is a $2 entrance fee if you're not staying at the lodge but it is well worth it for the view.

The best time to see the hot red lava pouring out of the active side is when the sun is setting (or has set) and I thought that such a sight would make a great photo opportunity. Unfortunately, the road to get there was dreadful and I really wasn't sure if the Almera would make it. I also knew I wouldn't be able to stay very long since there weren't any street lights to illuminate the ramshackle road. However, I did get some great shots at dusk and the next time I visit Fortuna, I will definitely be driving an SUV.

Over the next few days, I visited all of the La Fortuna/Arenal offerings; walking around the town square, traversing the hanging bridges and hiking down to the waterfall. I recommend spending time at all three. I discovered that the road to the waterfall is also best traveled by SUV. Additionally, the trail to get to the waterfall is also somewhat steep and worthy of wearing a good pair of hiking sandals or sneakers. Making it down to the base of the waterfall though was well worth the trek. It was a remarkable sight to see and with a swimsuit, you can also go for a refreshing dip in the river.

I decided late one afternoon to hike up the hill on the hotel's property to check out their observatory point. Mind you, I decided to do this at dusk despite the absence of lights along the hill. It was an amazing trip up to the vista point. I saw little ants walking with leaves on their backs, acres upon acres of open space and farmland as well as two adult horses and two foals just roaming freely, eating the local vegetation. The observatory area was beautiful.

It was nearly dark by the time I started my descent and since the hill is made up of volcanic rock it wasn't exactly a smooth path. In typical Chrissy fashion, I was busy looking for photo ops instead of scouting the ground for safe passage. Of course, I fell and fell hard, onto a large and fairly abrasive chunk of volcanic rock. As always, my priority was protecting my camera, which resulted in badly scratching up my left leg. There was a fair amount of blood and pain but I managed to hobble back down the hill to the hotel. Not that I had much choice. I was alone and I definitely wasn't going to stay out there all night.

Scars will fade and bodies will heal. I guess I shouldn't really worry all that much about the camera as it's been dropped out of a car window onto blacktop and it still works (again, I don't recommend trying that at home) but old habits die hard. I wouldn't say that I'm a clumsy person but I do seem to fall a lot, though mostly when I'm on trips. I had been to Monterey a few months earlier and fallen while walking on the rocks at the beach. It probably had something to do with the fact that I'm almost never wearing appropriate shoes for hiking (I refuse to give up my Keds). At any rate, my falls have made for some interesting scars and amusing stories, so I bear them with grace (full irony intended).

I only saw Troy one more time on that trip. He had left his sunglasses in the rental car and I dropped them off at his work my last afternoon in town. Of course, I made sure to dress it up to the nines, makeup and all, which is rare for me. I wanted to make a point. I had a green halter summer dress on and when I walked up to the front desk at Troy's work, he took a double take and told me, "Wow, you should always wear green. Your eyes are beautiful". He gave me a kiss and acted like nothing was wrong between us. I handed him his sunglasses and walked out the door, careful not to let him see the tears rolling down my face, lest it ruin my proud exit.

Leaving La Fortuna and on the way to the airport, I sent Troy a text…"Adios, mi amigo". He responded with, "Hasta luego". Until next time? Really? He just blew me off for four days, in his own town and he thought nothing was wrong? It would be months before we'd speak again after time and practicality had eased the hurt I was feeling. I knew that if I truly wanted to move to Costa Rica, it would be important to know people there. I decided that if nothing else, I would be gracious enough to allow Troy to be my friend.

## Chapter 7

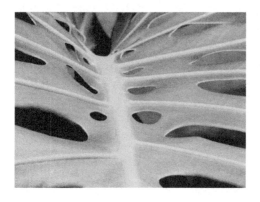

*Manuel Antonio-Playa Dominical*

January 2009

In San Jose, the rental car agent made a little small talk with me while he prepared my paperwork.

He asked, "Is this your first visit to Costa Rica?"
"No, it's my fourth visit!" I replied.
"Oh, well then, you are almost a Tica!"

We both laughed, but I liked the idea of becoming a Tica and giving up my US citizenship. When I told the story to Troy later that week, he was equally amused. It's still something we laugh about and on each subsequent trip I ask him, "Am I a Tica yet?"

I learned my lesson from the Almera, this time renting a SUV. It was a very large Mitsubishi Montero and I thought that it was funny that the couple next to me rented the same vehicle but I was given the larger of the two. I guess I was cuter (and more flirtatious).

After getting down the mountain with brakes that didn't seem to work, even in second gear, I wasn't as convinced that I had lucked out. The sun was setting, it was starting to rain and I still had to find the way to my hotel in Manuel Antonio before dark. I tried to call the hotel but the cell phone I had rented kept dying. Even plugging it into the car charger didn't help.

I drove by the street I was looking for six times without seeing the sign for Arenas del Mar Rainforest and Beachfront Resort and it was now dusk, with rain coming down on the windshield, making it that much more difficult to see the tiny hotel sign. The hotel's website had said, "4x4 vehicles recommended but not necessarily needed". If you read something like that in your travels, get a 4x4 vehicle. Actually, just get a 4x4 vehicle no matter what the website says.

I arrived at the road where the hotel is actually located, consisting of a steep hill without much visibility, only worsened by the pouring rain. As I pulled onto the road, I noticed another SUV coming up the hill. The road was only one lane and as I tried to back the car up onto the main road, the wheels started to spin out and I was rolling forward, down the hill. I can only imagine what the locals in the other car were saying about the girl who didn't know how to use a 4WD. There was no shoulder but they somehow managed to do a little offroading to get past me.

I checked in to my room and was assisted with my incredibly heavy luggage by an incredibly gracious bellboy (whom I offered a suitably weighty tip). Settling into the room, I was just in awe. It was nearly the size of the one-bedroom apartments I rented after college. The hotel had every amenity possible and a kind staff who were more than happy to accommodate any need or want. All of the difficulty getting there had been worth it. Paradise and adventure awaited me, though several baby land crabs grew impatient and camped out in my doorway. They were completely terrified but no matter how many times I helped them outside, they reappeared. I suppose they took their self appointed welcoming duties very seriously. Either way, I just hoped that none of them ended up in my suitcase.

Troy's hometown is just a few hours north of Manuel Antonio. When I planned my fourth trip to Costa Rica, he was working on the Nicoya Peninsula so we didn't think we'd be able to see each other. However, on my second day he called the hotel to tell me he had just been laid off and was back at home. The recession impacting the United States was affecting travel destinations as well. He had been working for a hotel and while it was the high season, there weren't enough tourists to sustain his position (and many other employees as well). So the good news was Troy and I could spend a few days together. The bad news was Troy was now out of a job.

I had thought this would be a solitary, meditative trip with a lot of time to focus on myself, but I was really happy to have the opportunity to spend a few days with Troy. It's also a nice perk when I can get him to drive.

That first morning was great. I had an incredible night's sleep and woke up feeling refreshed, watching the sunrise over Manuel Antonio Park. Breakfast was served in such large quantities that I didn't need to eat lunch (which is one way to save money while on holiday). Though there are many choices my typical meal, Gallo Pinto, consists of eggs, beans, rice, Turrialba cheese and tortillas. Everything is so fresh in Costa Rica, it's often straight off the farm and delicious. The cheese comes from a region in Costa Rica which I have yet to visit but plan to someday.

After breakfast, I decided to ask the front desk if I could change rooms. I really did want that ocean view. This isn't an uncommon phenomenon for me; I change rooms all the time. I was paying for an ocean view room and the hotel was more than accommodating in providing me with one.

I didn't enjoy packing and unpacking everything but the view from the new room was incredible which made it all worthwhile. The room also had a master bedroom which was separated from the living room by a door so I could wake up early and leave Troy to continue sleeping in while I enjoyed the sunrise from the balcony.

Only the bedroom itself had air conditioning but the other areas had a fan. (At the time of this printing, I've learned the hotel has installed air conditioning throughout the suite.) Troy hated it when I used the air conditioning; because it made it too cold for him but also because it's a waste of energy. He had a point but on really hot days, the fans can only do so much.

I then headed down to the beach for the day. One of the security guards at the beach pointed out a sloth who was lazily hanging from the branches, eating his lunch. I found watching the slot eat to be an incredibly relaxing experience. Everything is in slow motion with a sloth as they reach for their next leaf, pull it from the tree, place it in their mouth and then slowly chew it up.

I found myself taking deeper, slower breaths as I watched the sloth finish up and find a comfortable position on the branch to take a nap.

I vaguely wished I could grab a lounge chair and do nothing all day but I knew that I would be unhappy with myself it I didn't make use of the camera in my hand. I headed to the tide pools to seek out sea life. I found a number of interesting crabs and fish but was disappointed at the absence of starfish. I did get some great shots of the tree lined beach and green blue water.

After my beach time, I walked back up the hill to my room and passed another sloth on the way. I began to wonder if it was some kind of subtle reminder for me to slow down.

Later that afternoon, Troy called to make sure I was okay. He informed me that there had been an earthquake near Poas volcano registering 6.2 on the Richter scale. I'd been sitting on the beach when it happened and hadn't felt anything. Troy had felt it and the reports on the news indicated that it was fairly serious; there were several deaths, mass evacuations and rescue efforts being made.

I e-mailed my family to let them know I was okay (even though, as usual, the US media didn't report it in the States). My original travel plan was to visit Santa Barbara first, which is near Poas, and then go to Manuel Antonio. Had I kept to that plan, I would have been at the volcano at the time of the quake. I still find myself a little unsettled over this narrow escape. I'm grateful the universe brought me to Manuel Antonio first and has allowed me to keep up with my adventures.

After the shock and existential gratitude passed, my practical mind kicked in. I realized that I needed to find out the extent of the damage in Santa Barbara to determine if I needed to change my upcoming travels. I have to admit, I had a little fear about the idea of going to the volcano just a few days after a massive earthquake had hit the area. The front desk was kind enough to call my next hotel and they said all was well in their area. I was relieved, though the idea of staying a few more days at the beach had begun to grow on me.

I decided to schedule a bird watching tour for the morning before Troy was set to arrive, as I knew it was something he wouldn't really want to do. I woke up at 5:30 to go on the tour at 6:00. I arrived at the lobby and was so very grateful to see the freshly brewed coffee and light snacks. At about 6:20, I asked the concierge if the guide would be arriving soon. She then tried to call him but told me he wasn't answering the phone.

This was a classic example of the way Costa Ricans are so laidback. I love the laissez-faire, pura vida outlook; taking each day as it comes, even if it occasionally derails my own plans. "Oh well," I thought, when I realized I would not be going on the bird watching tour, "C'est la vie." I do sometimes wonder how long I would have sat there in the lobby waiting if I hadn't inquired though. Just because I appreciate the lifestyle doesn't mean I want to sit there waiting for someone who is never going to arrive!

When Troy and I spoke the day before about meeting in Jaco, he sounded shocked when I told him I'd meet him at KFC. I think there may have been a hearing or translation problem between "meet at" and "eat at" because he then said, "You want to meet me where?" I only chose KFC because I had passed several signs for it on the main road to Manuel Antonio and hoped that it would be easy to locate. I was happy to know he wasn't any bigger fan of the establishment than I was, but it was still so funny that he was so dismayed by my choice.

I find it incredibly sad to see the influence the United States has on other countries. On my drive to Manuel Antonio, I passed by numerous signs and billboards which let me know KFC, Quiznos and Subway could all be found in Jaco. I also passed large high-rise condominium buildings and there were many communities which looked frighteningly similar to the Orange County, California suburbs: Large, Mediterranean style homes built right next to each other, leaving no open space.

I wondered; What was there at one time? A large meadow? A small jungle? Birds, sloths, monkeys, and endangered species? Species that had not yet been discovered but were now removed from their habitat and forced to find new living spaces?

Just like when I was in Tamarindo and drove past the Subway and TCBY or flying into San Jose and seeing Denny's, I wondered...Is this really the kind of influence we want to have on other parts of the world? Don't we have other things to offer to them which would help them develop and grow into a prosperous nation? I know that the States has many things to offer that won't cause heart disease, obesity, diabetes and other serious health issues but I see little of that abroad.

When I picked up Troy, we stopped at the market in Quepos for nourishment (AKA cervezas) and I made him drive the rest of the way back to the hotel. He realized just how big of a favor that was once we arrived at the hotel's shoulder-less one lane road. At least it was sunny and dry for his attempt... I felt little compassion for his look of doubt. At this point, since I was sipping on a cold beer, enjoying the ride without any cares, I just giggled and replied, "Yep! This is it!"

Troy informed me that drinking in a moving vehicle was, "Okay", (meaning it's not really legal but everyone does it), so it's not an act of mine that I'd recommend that you take up. It wasn't my most responsible choice, but I was on vacation and trying to let loose a little. That's really all I can say for myself. He provided a similar explanation about marijuana usage but that one didn't tempt me. A beer on the road when I wasn't the one driving? That was just a little harder to pass up. Troy also tried to tell me that wearing my seat belt, which I always did but he doesn't like to do, was not required. One day I asked him why there were painted hearts with halos over them on the roads. He then had to explain to me that they served as a reminder to always wear your seatbelt and oh, yes, it was a law despite his lack of fondness for it.

Once Troy was settled, we headed down to the beach where the bar area was playing reggae music and the sun was just starting to set. We ordered nachos and beers and took in the view of the sun setting over the Pacific Ocean. While I knew Troy was worried about not having a job, I was enjoying having him here with me again.

Later that evening, we went out to the patio and sat on the lounge chairs. At one point, Troy took my hand and gestured for me to join him on his chair. It was so nice to lie in his arms, the back of my head resting on his chest, his arms wrapped around me. No words were needed at that moment as we listened to the waves crash on the shore below and looked up at the stars above us. And, of course, Bob was playing in the background from my iPod speakers. Perhaps we were more than friends but there was no hurry to define our relationship. We were simply two people enjoying all the beauty that Costa Rica has to offer.

The next morning we agreed to go to Manuel Antonio National Park, which is one of Costa Rica's most treasured parks. I had thought we'd go for a hike, eager to see wildlife and jungle. Perhaps I should have mentioned that to Troy but it didn't occur to me.

The road to get there doesn't really seem like one that would lead toward a National Park but Troy knew that it was, in fact, the way to go. As we approached the entrance we noticed there wasn't a designated parking area but there was a dirt lot off to the left. We parked there and told the young boy standing in the lot we'd like him to watch our car while we were in the park. We were sure not to give him any money until we returned per Troy's assertion that there wouldn't be an incentive for him to watch if he got money at the outset. It cost us $2 US dollars to have him watch the car, which is a pretty good deal.

If you make the trip, be advised that non-residents can enter the park for $10 while residents pay $2. It's a very popular destination so expect to wait in line as they only allow a certain amount of people to enter at one time.

Since Troy was the "local", I figured I'd let him be the tour guide and just follow along. The park (from the small part I saw) was a beautiful jungle and I'm sure there were lots of birds and other wildlife to view in the interior. But Troy had other plans...we were going to the beach.

The beach was breathtaking, incredibly pristine with white sand and water of a color you normally don't see on the Pacific Coast. The Caribbean Coast has clear turquoise blue water while the Pacific is often a darker shade. The beach was crowded and it was nice to see so many local people, instead of just tourists, enjoying their country's recreational areas. I hadn't brought my swimsuit as I thought we were hiking so I found a place that was partly shaded to sit while Troy basked in the sun. Even in the shade, it was still so hot so I opted to take a walk on a path that followed the beach but was mostly covered by trees.

Just a few feet away from all of the people enjoying the sunshine and warm water is where I found the monkeys swinging from the trees and running around the ground. Unlike the howlers, who generally don't come down from their treetops, the white faced monkeys scavenge thus why it's a good idea not to leave anything out that you don't want taken. It was so much fun to watch them, especially the little ones. There were several babies in the group and they were all playing with each other, in

what seemed like a game of tag, or perhaps it was hide and seek. Either way, they were chasing each other and rough housing, the perfect illustration for the term "monkeying around" in their very own jungle gym.

They have no fear so there were a few times when they came really close, looking at my camera, which was in front of my face, no doubt wondering if it was something they could grab and eat.

Being in the shade, I had my sunglasses on top of my head until I saw one of the older adults eyeing them. I immediately threw the glasses into my backpack as the lenses had my prescription in them and I would rather not find myself in need of a new pair. I saw one monkey jump from a tree onto a blanket which had someone else's picnic lunch on it, even though the people weren't around. The monkey grabbed a loaf of bread and ran back up the tree where he shared it with two of his friends. I cringed. It is so very important that any type of wildlife not be given human food. Researchers have found that wild animals are dying from human related diseases like heart disease and they're attributing it to the fact that people either leave food out for them to find or they are feeding them directly.

I recently heard a radio interview with people were talking about their travels to the Bahamas. They said that they were diving in the Caribbean Sea and in order to get the fish to approach them, they would squeeze cheez-wiz into the water. I was horrified to hear the story and when I later googled the topic, I found numerous other accounts of people saying the same thing. Don't even get me started on highly processed food which isn't even good for humans, being put out into the ocean…

There were signs posted in several key locations throughout the park. asking people not to use flash. But of course there was one person ignoring not just the signs but the request of his friend. I hadn't yet written this book, but if I could find him, I'd definitely give him my chapter outlining all of the reasons why his actions where irresponsible.

Shelving my annoyance with his lack of respect, I kept on down the path and came across a cute monkey family sitting on a tree branch. The mom was feeding the baby while the dad was inspecting the fur of the baby and cleaning her.

I forgot to mention this in earlier but Costa Rica and other Central American countries do have ticks. However, at least in Costa Rica, the ticks, at this time, do not carry Lyme disease. Thank goodness for one less thing to worry about.

Once I had my fill of the monkeys, I walked to another stretch of beach which was nearly deserted. I saw a "Jesus Christ lizard", aptly named because they can walk on water, or so I'm told. There were also a few mapaches (raccoons) running around the beach, scavenging for food like the monkeys.

Unfortunately, I have a bad habit of losing track of things on trips. I am a firm believer you should never intentionally leave things behind but somehow I lost my lipstick, the attachment for the telephoto, zoom and sun filter lens. That was a huge bummer. I'm not certain how or where I lost them. Perhaps a monkey got a hold of it at Manuel Antonio. He would have had to unzip my backpack but one never knows... monkeys are, after all, very smart primates. All I know is the photographs just won't be the same without the telephoto lens.

The next day we drove south to a surf beach that Troy really liked. The server at breakfast had told us the road was pretty bad but that with a 4x4, it would be manageable. The beach was forty-four kilometers, about twenty-six miles, from Manuel Antonio and it took us ninety minutes to get there thanks to the stellar road conditions.

However, it was totally worth the wild drive on the crazy roads, getting lost (which added another thirty minutes on top of the ninety) and not being able to see because of the dirt from the cars driving on the other side of the road.

Part of me was grateful that the roads were in such a bad state as it meant that fewer tourists would come to visit. I was also quite pleased that I had chosen to rent an SUV. In addition to the roads, flash flooding was also quite common in this area and while we didn't have to face that issue because it was summer, it just provided peace of mind not to have to think about it. Especially since a freak thunderstorm could always occur. Since we had the Montero, Troy was able to go between 40-50 mph for the most part although there were many times when we had to slow down because of dust, bumps and ditches.

Upon inspection, Playa Dominical proved to be a tiny little surf town. There were a few restaurants, a yoga studio and a very long stretch of beach. The surf was up that day and people, mostly locals, crowded onto the beach to catch a few waves and rays of sunshine. There wasn't any shade at the shore unless you left the sand for the tree-lined areas near the parking lot, so I was glad that I was better prepared that the day before with not just my swimsuit but sunscreen. Troy and I took turns playing in the water (it doesn't really matter what country you're in, you still can't leave your belongings unattended) and we took a nice walk on the beach together just before we left.

I had noticed a few big pieces of driftwood further down the beach so I took a longer walk to get to those. I have always been keen on driftwood...I often wonder what kind of story it carries...where did it come from and how did it end up there? When I was in my early 20's, my ex and I went to Santa Cruz after an El Niño storm and the beach was covered in driftwood. He picked up a piece, took out his Swiss army knife and carved our names in it with a heart around them. So sweet. It was one of his (few and far between) finer moments.

From where I stood with my prized driftwood, I could see my love sitting on the sand, soaking up the sun. While we had taken two towels with us from the hotel, he actually laid one out for me to sit on and then he rolled up the other so I could use it as a pillow if I wanted to lie down. I was touched by his thoughtfulness.

I wasn't looking forward to the long drive back to Manuel Antonio on the dirt roads but I was so happy he was with me. Not just because I like it when he drives and I can prop my feet up on the dash, enjoy the ride and check out the scenery but because it's so nice to have him in my life. We did pick up some nourishment for the ride back (AKA cerveza and chips) and other than the massive dirt storms; we really didn't run into any problems.

At breakfast that morning, we met a couple who recommended Ronny's Place as a location to watch the sunset and enjoy light appetizers and drinks. They weren't too sure how to describe the location of Ronny's but Troy said he'd figure it out. So on our way back to the hotel, Troy managed to find the road that led to Ronny's and it did turn out to be a spectacular view.

We sat outside on the cliff and watched as the sun went down while we enjoyed a few beers and dinner. The best part though was when a cat approached our table and hopped up onto Troy's lap.

Troy isn't really a cat person. He'll put up with them but he doesn't really like them. However this cat didn't care about any of that; he nuzzled his head into Troy's chest and made himself quite comfortable in his lap.

I was surprised Troy allowed him to rest there but perhaps he knew I was missing my cat and didn't want to upset me by being mean and throwing the cat off him (which I'm sure was a thought that went through his head).

Our last day at the beach (and together), we woke up to a beautiful sunrise. The skies were partly cloudy and tinged with golden hues from the rising sun. We woke up and had breakfast, then "took a sun". That's how Troy said "laid out" which I think is really cute and is an expression which I now regularly use. The tide was low and out so we were able to walk around the rocks. Troy had gone first and he called out to me to come meet him. I really should hire him to be my scout as he had found a great tide pool area for me to photograph. I love that about him. He knows me so well, knows what I'm looking for and makes a point to help me with the work I'm doing. I should also mention here that he's a pretty good photographer as well. After our beach time, we headed back up to the room to pack and check out.

Troy told me he'd drive me to San Jose and then he'll take a bus back to his hometown from there. It was totally out of his way but he knew how much I didn't like driving so it was a nice offer. The sadness at the thought that we would be parting was starting to settle on my shoulders like a weight... I only had three more nights in Costa Rica and I would have loved to have had him stay with me. I also know Troy really doesn't like the inland portions of his country. They're too cold for him and as I'd find out, they're a little too cold for me as well. I was surprised I needed to wear socks in the evenings as normally, I don't wear any for the entire trip.

As we drove out of Manuel Antonio, Troy told me that he wanted to show me another favorite surf spot, Playa Hermosa. There are two Playa Hermosa's in Costa Rica: one in Puntarenas (where we were) and one in Guanacaste on the Nicoya Peninsula. The one in Puntarenas is famous for its surfing and was even chosen as the location for the 2009 Billabong World Surf Competition. I had attempted to get tickets to fly down for the competition but the hotels were either booked or ridiculously expensive, making the trip completely impractical.

There wasn't much surf that day but the one thing I do remember is the black sand. I don't know why I can't remember to wear my sandals on black sand beaches but there I was, shoeless, with the soles of my feet burning as I tried to run, hop really, back to the car.

With Troy driving, I was able to relax as we headed back over the mountain. It was so nice to actually take in the scenery and see the beautiful countryside. The sadness returned though as we approached San Jose. I knew our time was once again coming to an end. I tried to look out the window because the tears were welling up in my eyes. I didn't want Troy to leave but I also knew I didn't have a choice. When we got to a bus stop near the airport, we stopped the car and said our goodbyes. We kissed and hugged as a tear rolled down my face. Troy saw I was upset, he wiped the tears from my face and he then kissed me on the forehead, telling me he loved me and to be safe for the rest of my trip.

I know that Shakespeare wrote that parting was sweet sorrow, but truly I think it must have been a typo as this was bittersweet at best.

## Chapter 8

*Santa Barbara-Sarchi-Poas*

The hotel I stayed at, Finca Rosa Blanca (translated: White Rose Farm), was located in the hills above San Jose and was a beautiful, eclectic property... definitely not a typical hotel. Local artisans made most of the unique furnishings and woodwork. I knew I would be in good hands as the same company as Arenas del Mar and Harmony managed the hotel. As always, the food was excellent and everyone was very accommodating.

At most of the hotels I visit, it seems like the staff members are always a little surprised when I show up alone. They don't seem to understand why or how a thirty-something year old single female would be traveling alone in a foreign country (even Troy has expressed confusion about that). However, one thing that is great about traveling alone is I get to meet and talk with the staff so much more than I would if I was traveling with others. I love getting to know the people who work at the hotels and the tours. It's such a great opportunity for me to understand who they are as I'm traveling in their country and really learn about and appreciate the cultural differences. It helps me see the world from a different perspective and I appreciate that so much.

The earthquake that happened the previous week turned out to have caused more damage than expected and the front desk told me that they did not believe Poas would be open during my stay. I was further disappointed because this new information meant that I wouldn't be able to get to the Sarapiquai Suspension Bridges either, though I supposed that after an earthquake, the potential aftershocks would render traversing a suspension bridge rather dangerous.

A change of plans was in order. I decided to try a bird watching tour, since my previous one fell through. I met the guide, Manolo, the day before my tour and felt positive about the likelihood of him actually showing up.

Troy told me if I did go to Poas (as there is still a chance they could reopen it before I left), to keep my keys in my hand and if I heard a siren or other loud noises, to run back to the car and get the heck out of the area. That didn't sound even remotely encouraging, especially since Poas is located in a remote area of a mountain. However, my inner Pippi Longstocking thought it sounded like a great adventure so I hoped that I'd get the chance to make it Poas, safety be damned.

My second day in Santa Barbara was so eventful, starting with a rolling aftershock at 1 in the morning. I was reminded of how much I don't like earthquakes, especially in the middle of the night, in a strange bed in a foreign country. My mind raced. Do I get up? Where do I go? There weren't any doorways that looked structurally comforting. There were beams in the ceiling and the main entrance had a huge glass skylight, covering the entire roof (which under normal circumstances would be quite nice). Should I go outside? The rolling stopped within twenty seconds, but my mind didn't calm and allow me to sleep until 3 a.m.

At 5:30a.m. I dragged myself out of bed to go on the bird watching tour (which would have been so much better if I hadn't lost my telephoto lens attachment in Manuel Antonio). I noticed a gigantic wasp nest hanging off the tree outside my room which didn't excite me to say the least. However, on my tour I saw a colorful mot mot bird and learned so much from Manolo about the various species of birds, their habitats and lives. My personal favorite tidbit of information was that cattle egret hang out with cows because when cows move, they press their hooves down into the soil releasing insects which the egrets eat.

Breakfast consisted of my routine favorite, Gallo Pinto. (Of course!) The dish was also accompanied by a delicious mixed fruit juice, muffin and fruit plate, though I realized that as much as I like the way star fruit look, I really don't like how they taste.

Suitably nourished, I set off on a fantastic Sustainable Plantation coffee tour. I learned on this tour that coffee is actually a fruit. I'd always wanted to go on one and this was my first opportunity. It was two hours long and included a tour of the plantation, the history of coffee, what makes a sustainable, organic coffee and why it's different, why it's needed and why it's difficult for small growers to convert over to organic from conventional. Leo, my guide, and I also discussed why Starbucks is good (they brought worldwide attention to coffee) and why they are very, very bad... but I already knew the answer to this question. Currently, only 5% of Starbucks coffee is sustainable, organic and/or fairly traded. Starbucks could make such an impact on the lives of coffee growers around the world by implementing more fairly traded coffee into their stores. I have chosen not to support Starbucks since 2006 and now only purchase my coffee (in my travel mug, mind you) from local coffee shops that I know serve fairly traded and organic coffee drinks.

The tour came with a coffee tasting (sort of like wine tasting) which was both interesting and educational. I learned many Costa Rican coffee farmers add sugar to the coffee, before it's put in the bag and sold. Leo told me it can be used to make bad coffee taste a little better but, historically, it is also a traditional coffee making method.

Important tip...you know you're drinking a good brand of coffee if it still tastes good when it's gone cold. If it tastes bad when cold, then it wasn't a good coffee to begin with. Leo said almost any coffee will taste good when it's hot.

Around noon I drove to Sarchi and found the town plaza and church but couldn't find the area with the old ox carts, which Sarchi was known for. I tried to get into the church but it appeared to be locked. I'd never been to a church that was locked before and wondered if it was some kind of sign.

I took a photo of the plaza, which had one gigantic ox cart and the church and decided to chance a trip to Poas in hopes that they had reopened the Park. A little over an hour later, I found myself lost, despite the assistance of GPS. I did pass by a sugarcane plantation, which was kind of neat, but also a good number of ambulances and police cars. If the locked church was a sign, then certainly the content of the traffic didn't bode well for me.

As I made my way up the mountain, a warning sign on the car dashboard lit up: A/T temp. I thought it meant "automatic transmission temperature" but I couldn't know for sure since there wasn't a manual in the glove compartment (and it probably would have been in Spanish and therefore less than helpful to me). I checked the temperature gauge but it looked normal, right at the half way point. At that point I was in the middle of nowhere with no one in sight so I don't bother to check either cell phone because if they didn't have service, I'd probably begin to panic. I finally arrived at the Poas Park entrance where the gates were still closed and locked, and I turned around to head back to the safety of my hotel.

Eventually, the warning light turned off on its own as I headed back down the mountain in 2nd gear. I reprogrammed the GPS to return to Santa Barbara but it took me a different route than I came in on originally. The road was really damaged. This was the area that got hit with major landslides and damaged homes and businesses. There were several areas where traffic was stopped while forklifts and heavy machinery removed buildings and landslides from the road. I passed by two Red Cross camps, one of which I got out of the car to photograph. The police stopped me and wouldn't let me enter the camp but did let me continue on with my photography.

Once I was back on the road, the GPS led me to turn onto an unpaved road. The road took me through beautiful coffee plantations and followed a lovely stream. At one point, I parked the car to take a photo and while doing so, a truck with several people, who looked like they were just finishing up work in the coffee fields, stopped to see if I was okay. I thought that was really kind for them to stop, especially since I'm sure they were tired after a long day's work in the summer sun. I finally found my way to my hotel at 5:00 p.m. after many missed streets since the location of my hotel wasn't on GPS.

I hadn't had any lunch so I decided on an early dinner. I selected a vegetarian sandwich with fresh fruit and a Bavaria Gold. This was honestly one of the best sandwiches I had ever eaten. Yes, I was starving, but biting into this delicious sandwich made me forget all of the craziness I had endured. That was nothing short of a miracle...

I woke the next morning to a beautiful sunrise, rays peaking through the pine trees, which were just outside my balcony and falling in my room in pretty patterns. It's surprising to me to see pine trees in Costa Rica. I normally associate pine trees with snow (and palm trees with Costa Rica) but I was told they could be found, indigenously, in the higher, cooler elevations throughout the country.

I started off my last full day here with a tour of the hotel's property and their sustainability practices. They were the first boutique hotel in Costa Rica to receive "5 Leaves" from the Certificate of Sustainable Tourism organization. Just as a reference, The Four Seasons in Papagayo is still at 4 Leaves.

At breakfast I splurged, choosing whole wheat French toast instead of Gallo Pinto. It wasn't so much the toast I wanted but the syrups that came with it: brown cane sugar (the thickest syrup I've ever seen), coconut syrup and raspberry. The French toast was excellent but with the syrups, divine.

I finished up the morning with a tour at the local medicinal herb and botanical garden in Santa Barbara. My guide told me that he believes any disease or health issue can be cured by an herb or plant, which was really fascinating to learn about in greater depth. There was one very pretty plant, which I learned had hallucinogenic properties. Just standing next to it at sunset for twenty minutes could make you feel as though you were drunk. I remembered seeing a similar plant outside my bedroom at the villa and giggled at the thought of hanging out near it and saving money on my bar tab. He also had me taste many of the plants, including a sweet lemon, a leaf of the stevia plant and lastly dragon's blood, which was an anesthetic and dried up my tongue the instant it touched it. At the end of the tour, my guide's wife brought out Tamarindo juice and crackers with local cheese and decorated with pretty edible flowers.

This was my first experience with Tamarindo juice and I couldn't get enough of it. It's a delicious drink that is both slightly sweet and sour and it quenched my thirst in the hot summer sun. This is not the same "Tamarind" soda you can buy in US stores and Mexican restaurants. I'm not even sure if those bottles of "juice" have any actual fruit in them. I munched on the snack as I wished that the United States would focus more on natural healing through plants and herbs rather than popping pills all the time. The plants and herbs just seemed like a much healthier alternative to the synthetic creations regularly prescribed by doctors back home.

I spent my afternoon walking around the hotel grounds, soaking up the sunshine, taking a siesta and saying goodbye to the friends I had made. My soak in the jacuzzi tub was a perfect end to a beautiful day.

On my final day during this trip, I'm happy to report I didn't fall once, nor did I lose any more items. However, I did step into an anthill in the morning and got bit terribly, which was rather painful, but other than that incident, I had an insect friendly trip which didn't require the use of my Burt's Bees repellent. I wish I could claim that the lack of insect trouble was due to my status as an "almost Tica" and the bugs are no longer attracted to me but in truth, there are a lot less bugs in summer since there is a lot less rain. Whatever the reason though, I'm pleased when any trip to the Rich Coast wraps up with fewer run ins with insects which put this down as a great trip despite the natural disasters and changed plans.

## Chapter 9

*San Jose-Osa Peninsula-San Jose*

May 2009

Originally I'd planned to go back to Costa Rica in November but after the 32 degree morning in California, wondering why on Earth I was in the States, I realized that I wanted to go back much sooner. I wanted to visit the Osa Peninsula and called Troy to see if he'd be up for the trip and whether or not he could afford the plane ticket to Osa. He said he'd try but he didn't know if he'd be working (it was now mid-February and he still hadn't found a new job). He supposed that if he was working in May, he wouldn't be able to take time off. We agreed to just play it by ear.

I didn't have any plans for this eleven-day trip other than to stay at Lapa Rios for five nights so I was really hoping Troy would be able to come along and we could go off and explore the country during the other six evenings. Normally, I plan my trips minute by minute, always know where I'm going to stay and how I'm getting there. This is a very logical way to travel but I decided to let my inner "almost Tica" embrace the Pura Vida and be a little more spontaneous.

Troy was supposed to meet me at the airport when I arrived in San Jose but something came up. He did contact one of his friends, Manuel, who runs a taxi service in San Jose to take me from the airport to the hotel. While the act was thoughtful, I ended up paying Manuel twice what I would have paid the hotel shuttle. Though I was a little irritated, I was more anxious that perhaps Troy wasn't going to show up at all. He wasn't always totally reliable. I definitely was not as into the ever changing plans and going with the flow as he was. I was relieved when, shortly before sunset, I got a call to let me know that he was in the lobby. I ran out to meet him and immediately fell into his arms. We drank a beer in the room as we spent some time catching up and all my irritation with the change in plans washed away as I drank in his presence. Pura Vida is just fine when it swings in my direction.

Later that night, we decided to take a walk down the road to the local mall. This was my first (and only) experience of a Costa Rican mall and I found it disappointingly similar to malls in the states. I was again saddened at how we've brought so much of our influence to other countries. It was a Friday night and the mall was filled with people. Consumerism and the need for more stuff hung in the air like a fog as people walked around with their new purchases. Troy, as usual, ran into someone he knew. We had dinner at a pizza place and though it was a fast food restaurant, which added to my displeasure with the pervasiveness of my own culture, it was actually very tasty.

The next morning, we were up early to catch our flight to Osa. We were going to be flying on Nature Air, the first "carbon neutral" airline in the world; meaning that a portion of the ticket price goes to creating carbon offsets. I appreciated the opportunity to pay some of the external costs that I referred to previously. Nature Air supports reforestation projects in Costa Rica with the carbon credits earned from ticket purchases. Since most airlines don't include the carbon offsets in the ticket price, there are organizations that you can purchase carbon credits from independently, in order to take personal responsibility for the pollution you are causing while traveling but for this flight, I was happy to not have to be mindful about the extra step.

I was nervous about taking a puddle jumper flight, not because of the size of the plane but for the simple fact that everything had to be weighed... including people. I was so horrified that I was going to have to get on a scale with Troy standing by my side. I may take great care of my body through yoga and traipsing up and down lava rocks but I still wasn't thrilled at letting my boyfriend (for lack of a better word) know a number for my weight. Blessedly, the universe was looking out for me in my moment of girlish panic because the scale at the counter we went to wasn't visible to anyone but the agent. If had we gone one counter over, I would not have been so fortunate. I thanked my lucky stars and did a happy dance... in my head. I'm pretty sure that a real happy dance would have called into question my desire not to have my weight seen in the first place and that would have been yet another thing Troy didn't get about me.

After check-in we went to a park outside the airport and drank a few beers that we had leftover from the night before.

It was 7:30 in the morning but we were on vacation and a little nervous about the upcoming plane ride. Out of boredom or silliness or an elaborate blend of the two, Troy decided to go hug a tree while we were passing the hour until our flight. I wondered if the term tree hugger carried the same connotation in Spanish that it does in the states, but I guessed not.

Back in the airport, we had to go through security so that they could search our carry-on bags. Normally, the search just consists of opening a backpack or purse and peering inside, however this particular agent went so far as to open Troy's sunglass bag where he had stashed a joint. I held my breath for a moment, knowing that the marijuana was technically illegal but hoping that the agent held to Troy's "It's OK" philosophy. Either the agent didn't care or he didn't see it because he let us pass without incident.

The flight to Osa was uneventful. No turbulence, the pilot didn't fall asleep (as I later found out had happened on a friend's flight to Osa) though we did land on an airstrip next to a cemetery which was a sobering though while landing in a tiny place in the middle of nowhere. Troy and I were greeted by the friendly Lapa Rios staff whom promptly offered us coconut water (inside an actual coconut) and two cold beers, perhaps well aware of the effects of landing near the cemetery.

Lapa Rios is located at the edge of the Osa Peninsula, where the Pacific Ocean meets the Golfo Dulce (translated: the sweet gulf). Mostly, we drove past farmland and jungles, off-roading a few times over small rivers, much to my inner Pippi's excitement. With the exception of the farms, the Peninsula truly was paradise.

The Osa Peninsula is considered the most biologically diverse region in the world, given the abundance of types of flora and fauna in the area and the Peninsula's small size. There are numerous species living there, many of them are endangered such as: spider monkeys, scarlet macaws, whale sharks, jaguars, pumas and howler monkeys. Organizations like the Nature Conservancy are actively working to protect the area from deforestation and the animal species from extinction due to poachers and habitat loss. Whales from both the North and the South migrate to the area and I was told this is the only place where this happens from both hemispheres.

The Golfo Dulce is home to large pods of wild dolphins (200 in just one pod!), mangroves, coral reefs, sea turtles and beautiful fish, including a zebra moray eel, which I spotted while snorkeling. Both sides of the Gulf have protected national parks: Corcovado and Piedras Blancas. There is also the second longest left hand surf break in the world on Osa, located in the small town of Pavones, near the border of Panamá.

Most of the roads are dirt, which helps with maintaining a low population density, allowing the environment to dominate, rather than people. There are both primary and secondary rainforests, the air is fresh and clean, the water is clear, and the weather is a tad rainy. The average rainfall is 160-280 inches. By comparison, I think my region of Northern California received about twenty-five inches this past year.

Fortunately for Troy and I, it only rained at night and mostly on the other side of the Gulf. From the deck of our balcony, we were able to watch spectacular lightning and thunder shows every night.

We were greeted at the lodge and given refreshing fruit drinks as well as reusable water bottles. I explained that Troy and I both had our own stainless steel bottles but thanked the staff for their environmental consideration. The eco-lodge is a private reserve that has almost 1,000 acres of primary and secondary rainforest. Primary rainforest is one that is in its original condition, never having been cut down. It generally has a full canopy and unless a tree has fallen, very little light gets through to the forest floor. It also tends to be more biologically diverse than secondary forests. I found it very comforting to know that the land at Lapa Rios is protected in perpetuity, even if the property is sold to new owners.

When we got to our room, I noticed that there were two queen beds instead of one king and they each had mosquito netting. I wasn't excited about either situation and wondered how they would bode for the days to come. I knew we would be too hot in the mosquito netting with both of us in one bed so separate beds were in our future. This wouldn't have been such an inconvenience if Troy didn't snore. With him sleeping in a separate bed, it would become much more difficult to sleep peacefully as I wouldn't be able to push him into a non-snoring position. I was also nervous about the bug situation if mosquito netting was required. While visually it can look a little like a romantic canopy letting lovers escape the outside world, it can actually do exactly the opposite if you catch a glimpse of all of the insects on the outside.

The room was so beautiful with its breathtaking view. It featured double sinks, a separate bathroom area for the toilet and shower with an extra large screened in window and separate cold and warm showerheads. Besides the two beds, there was a small desk in one corner and two chairs in another. The patio area was huge with an outdoor shower, hammock, table and two chairs as well as two lounge chairs. (I highly recommend asking for Bungalow 4).

Lapa Rios was a place to let everything go and just breathe. There were no televisions, phones, cell service or internet access. Like Finca Rosa Blanca and Harmony (and as of 2010, Arenas del Mar as well), they have a 5 Leaf designation from the Certificate of Sustainable Tourism organization and are always actively working on improving their sustainability practices, their commitment to the community and the environment and to educating others on ways to make a difference in the world. Their mission statement is, "A forest left standing is more valuable than one cut down". Those are just some of the reasons I chose the reserve for my lodging.

Another notable thing about our stay at Lapa Rios was the food, which in addition to being some of the best I have ever had was also sourced in a way that I found inspiring. While much of the food comes from local farms, some products are brought in from San Jose since Lapa Rios is a very remote location. The food is brought to the Peninsula by one of the lodge's Land Rovers which are fueled by biodiesel gasoline, creating less of an impact on the environment. Since it's about an eight-hour drive from San Jose, dinner orders are placed during the breakfast meal. The dinner menu is set by each day of the week and each option is exceptional, offering a soup/salad, entrée and dessert. Their cocktails are also highly recommended. The chefs are from the local area and self-taught. It was a beautiful example of how passion and determination will allow you to succeed at anything your heart truly desires.

Here are a few of my favorite meals copied from their menu, sans pictures.

Breakfast:

- Lapa Pupusa (this was my favorite): Two homemade corn tortillas sandwiched with black beans and cheddar cheese. Topped with a fried egg and avocado.

Lunch:
- Garden Tica Salad: Crisp greens, crunchy vegetables and local flavors, including palm hearts, white Turrialba cheese and pejibaye make a unique fresh salad. Add grilled chicken, fish or sautéed tofu. Served with your choice of homemade dressings: Papaya Seed, Caesar, Balsamic Vinaigrette or Sesame-soy . Pejibaye, vitamin/mineral-rich starchy plum-size Osa-endemic palm fruits, boiled then peeled
- Portobello Mushroom Sandwich: Sautéed Portobello mushrooms, grilled sweet red chiles and onions, topped with melted Mozzarella cheese on toasted Ciabatta bread.

Dinner:

- Hearts of Romaine Macadamia Nut Salad: Honey-glazed macadamia nuts and crumbled Feta cheese top crisp hearts of romaine, drizzled with balsamic-garlic dressing. Best enjoyed in hand.
- Costa Rican Portobello and Spinach Risotto: Risotto made with Portobello mushrooms, fresh spinach, basil and topped with Parmesan cheese.
- Gnocchi with Pumpkin and Macadamia: Potato gnocchi with a honey-roasted squash purée filling and served with a macadamia nut sauce.

And then the desserts:
- Lapa Rios Mud Cake: Rich chocolate-banana cake served warm with vanilla ice cream and a passion fruit-butter sauce. Maracuyá (passion fruit) are native

to Central America, its flowering vines stretching meters along forest floors. The seasonal fruit is sweet and acidic, a perfectly balanced tropical perfume.
- Chocolate and Cajeta Cheesecake: A delicious cheesecake topped with cajeta and chocolate sauce Cajeta is a traditional tico dessert-like candy made from sweetened condensed milk.

They do offer meat dishes but of course I passed on those. Even if you do eat meat, I encourage you to try these incredible vegetarian options. One less meal with meat in it will make me feel like I have accomplished something but more importantly, you might find a new favorite that you wouldn't have otherwise.

The first two days Troy and I spent exploring the beach and playing in the water. It's a rocky beach, even in the water, and didn't feel great under my toes so I spent much of my time reading under the shade of a beautiful Almendra tree while Troy swam. We also met Amanda and Aaron, a lovely young couple from Missouri, and we were able to talk them into joining us on our day-long activity the next day.

Unfortunately, the next morning, Amanda wasn't feeling well but she was a good sport and continued with us on the tour. (She was most likely experiencing morning sickness as seven months later, she gave birth to a sweet baby girl, Ada Jane.) I can only imagine how Amanda must have felt about the bumpy ride on the rough, dirt road or the choppy boat ride that followed but she was always in a positive mood, making the most of it. After the less than pleasant travel we were able to find the dolphins that lived in the Golfo Dulce. Since they were wild, there were no guarantees, but we were fortunate. We also had the "WOW" experience to see a thirty foot whale shark. I was incredibly grateful that I was able to see these beautiful creatures play in their wild habitat.

After our dolphin encounter, we visited an animal sanctuary. When we first arrived and disembarked from the boat, a monkey came up to me and sat directly behind me with her back to me. We were told when they do that they want their backs to be scratched. When I reached down to scratch her, she was visibly happy and even pointed with her hands where she wanted me to rub her.

As we were given a tour of the property, two of their spider monkeys, which were very friendly, hopped up onto people to be carried around. They didn't just want to be held in our arms; they also liked to sit on shoulders. These were big, fully grown monkeys, not like little Sophie at Capitan Suizo so they were heavy but we were told not to try to carry them, just to allow them to hold on, as that is how they would have held on to their mother.

We also got to watch as one of the monkeys tried to get into the cage of another animal. The cage was locked but the monkey was literally hanging from the chain link fence, trying to pick the lock. Thankfully, its attempts were unsuccessful as the center had intentionally kept the animal hidden from public view, hoping to be able to release it back into the wild with as little human imprinting as possible.

Once we were back aboard the boat we set off for a snorkeling location. Thanks to the torrential rainfall the night before, the water wasn't as clear as I would have liked but it was still fun to get in the warm water and swim with the fish. After my first snorkeling experience, I explained to the guide that all I wanted was the eye mask. Everyone on the boat looked at me in a confused way and couldn't understand why I didn't want the entire ensemble of snorkeling equipment. I stood my ground knowing that I would be quite content with just the mask and silently hoping that we could get into the water and stop making a big deal out of it.

The absence of the breathing piece of the snorkel equipment did require a little more energy on my part to hold my breath but it was worth it. I could dive down without having water get into the tube and I was thankful for my expanded lung capacity thanks to teaching yoga. It was quite exhausting though and I was definitely ready for lunch and a nap on our deck when we returned to Lapa Rios. Just before we got back into town however, the guide took us on a quick tour into a mangrove. The tide was low and the boat wasn't able to go too far in but it was nice to see another kind of jungle and the birds and trees that lived there. Aaron thought he saw a crocodile but it dove below the surface before we were able to see it.

Before hiking up the hill for dinner, we decided to try out the outdoor shower. It was definitely a new experience to be showering outside in nature (and also a little romantic). Harmony also had an outdoor shower but I never really thought to use it. Next time...

The next morning, I woke up early to do my yoga practice on the deck as the sun was rising. It had rained all night and the air felt so fresh and clean. Troy was still sleeping when I finished and I decided to join him. As I opened the mosquito netting, he hazily woke up and opened his arms to me so that I could curl up next to him

After a delicious breakfast, Aaron and Amanda met up with us again to go on the Lapa Rios waterfall hike. As we entered the rainforest, our guide, Alberto, reminded us we would be entering the homes of the wildlife and plants on this tour and to have the utmost respect for all that surrounded us. I have never forgotten what he said as it really made an impact on how I viewed the environment we were entering as well as each place I have visited since.

Alberto was well versed in the different types of flora and fauna we were seeing and told us various uses for the trees and plants as we walked past them. We crossed over several streams and a few times I had to sit on my bottom in order to get down several little hills that were wet and muddy from the rainstorm the night before.

The hike took us to two beautiful, crystal clear waterfalls, which were quite cold... refreshing and much appreciated after the hike.

Later that afternoon, I went on a free sustainability tour the hotel was offering and Troy stayed back and took a sun at the pool. Learning about the environmental practices the EcoLodge had in place was so important to me. I already knew quite a bit because I thoroughly read through their website before arriving but I also learned some interesting new things such as the fact that the property hung laundry to dry rather than using a dryer. They also supported the local community by hosting nightly events showcasing local artisans.

One practice I was not a fan of was the use of pigs for methane gas. I understood that they were trying to reduce their reliance on carbon fuels however, as an animal advocate, I was concerned about the small space the large pigs were housed in and I hoped they would soon find a way to capture the gas while still allowing the pigs space to roam outside.

At the end of the tour, I was able to plant a tree in the rainforest. While I'm sure I'll never be able to find the specific one that I planted, knowing that I contributed to the reforestation of this beautiful Peninsula was a gift in itself. I dedicated the tree to my nephew, Justin, who I hoped I would be able to bring to Lapa Rios at some point to show him this little piece of protected paradise.

On our last morning at Lapa Rios, Troy and I got into a fight. Looking back, it's still something I can't believe we were arguing about. The fight centered on whether or not to use protection and since I believe that unprotected sex has no place outside of a committed relationship, we were at odds with each other. Due to this point of contention, Troy decided to end our sexual relationship. I was completely surprised by his abrupt decision, especially since neither of us had any condoms at Harmony and he had still wanted to spend every night with me. I really wasn't sure what to do with his decision and what it would mean for any future time together.

# Chapter 10

*San Jose-Las Juntas de Abangares-Monteverde-Tamarindo-San Jose*

The ride back to Puerto Jimenez and the flight to San Jose were very, very quiet. I was upset, angry and annoyed and at the same time, trying to figure out what I was going to do for the next five days. I wasn't sure if Troy would be leaving me like he did in Fortuna. I was filled with disappointment that my attempt to go with the flow had left me with no plans, when having them would have felt comforting in the midst of the uncertainty. Troy did end up staying with me for the rest of the trip, but I have to say the remainder of the trip lacked a certain sweetness that I normally felt when traveling in Costa Rica.

Outside of the airport, we met our driver from the rental car agency and headed into San Jose. The counter agent checked us in and was nice enough not to charge us for a second driver. We were renting a Montero again which was good since our newly contrived plan was to head to Monteverde the following day. Troy dropped me off at the hotel so that he could run an errand with a friend. I was fine with the time alone as I hadn't slept much the last few days due to Troy's snoring and I was still angry with him about the whole condom issue but I knew I needed to let it go.

I sent emails to my two best friends to explain the changes in my traveling relationship. I felt comforted by their reassurances of love and support, which brought a little bit of sunshine back into my world. I went to the bar and had a light lunch, then laid out at the pool, waiting for Troy to return.

Later that night, we met up with Troy's friend, Manuel, who had picked me up from the airport, and his wife at a reggae bar in San Jose. Manuel had held onto my extra luggage for me that I couldn't take with me on the puddle jumper. Occasionally, Troy and Manuel went outside together and I tried to make conversation with Manuel's wife but she didn't know much English and I didn't know much Spanish. We made do and mostly, I just did a lot of people watching.

The next day, Troy and I drove to Monteverde. From San Jose, it's about a four hour drive. We would be passing through his hometown and decided to stop at his house so he could pick up some clean clothes and show me around his town.

While at Lapa Rios, I had asked Troy why we had never traveled to his hometown together. He indicated that the places I chose to stay in Costa Rica led him to believe that I wouldn't appreciate his town. I do tend to stay at high-end hotels but as I mentioned before, that is mostly a safety precaution for when I am traveling alone and my desire to stay in establishments with superior environmentally conscious practices in place. Since I never know how long Troy will stay with me, or if he's even going to show up, I choose to stay at nicer hotels. I could tell Troy didn't understand either reason and so I tried to assure him I would love to see where he lived and that my home in California is nothing special. I was saddened that he thought I would judge him since I try to be so conscientious of respecting people.

Las Juntas de Abangares is a small town, about one and a half hours south of Liberia. The town has all of the usual Costa Rican attributes...a school, community center, sports center (where they hold rodeos in which Troy participated when he was younger), Catholic church, futbol field, basketball court and local eateries. Troy's mom didn't speak any English but she warmly welcomed me into her home and immediately went into the kitchen to prepare us a pitcher of carrot lime juice. I really liked Troy's home; I thought the size was perfect, it had simple furnishings and was very comfortable. There was a nice yard with trees, tropical flowers growing and of course, a hammock.

After leaving his mom's house, Troy wanted to show me the mines, which were located just outside of his town. No longer in use, they were now a part of the town's history, open to the public for hiking and educational purposes. While on the hike, we were caught in a severe thunderstorm but I didn't mind and everything dried quickly.

We had a delicious lunch afterwards at a lodge up the road and then began our ascent up the mountain to

Monteverde. Monteverde is only eighteen miles from Las Juntas but it's about an hour and a half drive with photo breaks. The all-dirt road was very winding at times and as usual, we came across large animals (at least this time, it was with the owner!)

Troy's cousin owned a small bed and breakfast there as well as a pizzeria so we were pretty set up for the next few days. Monteverde is a cloud forest outside of Santa Elena and we experienced heavy, and very cold, rain and thunderstorms while we were there. After just a day and a half of the rain, I decided we'd leave after the second night and head to Playa Tamarindo for one night to soak up a little sun before I had to return to San Jose.

I highly recommend visiting the Monteverde Cloud Forest Reserve, which is a beautiful jungle for hiking. We were fortunate to get an early start that morning as the rain didn't start to fall until we were just finishing our hike around 11 a.m. It is also known for being a place to view the Quetzal bird however we missed out because we were not visiting during the correct season.

Troy had visited the Reserve during a field trip when he was at University Latina and he decided to take me on a trail that led to the Continental Divide. For the most part, the hike was pretty easy. There were a few steep areas but overall, it was a leisurely hike in a beautiful rainforest. There were many trails to choose from but I would imagine you see much of the same, no matter which one you select.

While the morning was sunny, there was a haze over the outlying valleys and we weren't able to see much. On a clear day you can see both the Pacific Ocean to the West and the Caribbean Sea to the East. Just outside of the reserve was a small hummingbird garden. The hummingbirds were all wild but the reservists do leave out feeders for the birds to enjoy. There are also lots of flowers if you want to get a more natural photograph.

We had lunch at the Morpho restaurant and once again, I got meat on my plate. It really is difficult to get servers to understand the word vegetarian. Often, they think it just means you don't eat red meat but chicken or fish are okay. I also tried the drink, guanabana en leche. A friend at work had told me about it prior to this visit and insisted that I find a place that served it. The drink was good but I prefer Tamarindo juice.

Two other noteworthy restaurants in Santa Elena are The Treehouse (where a tree is growing through the middle of the restaurant) and Johnny's Pizzeria. The Treehouse had live music, a pleasant environment and the food was good. Troy's cousin's restaurant, Johnny's Pizzeria, is located just outside of town on the way to the Reserve. Despite the name, it is a full Italian restaurant and everything we ordered was delicious. We had a bottle of Pinot from Cono Sur (South America) and while I normally drink beer in Costa Rica, this was a very nice wine to accompany the Italian meal. Johnny gave us special treatment, as well as a huge discount, but even if he hadn't, it's still a place I recommend for lunch or dinner.

After the bottle of wine and the after-dinner drink which Johnny insisted we have, I was feeling a little buzzed but we decided to go to a local bar and have a few beers. I think part of me was trying to drink away my sadness that Troy and I were together but not together. Needless to say, the next morning, I was feeling a little hungover thanks to my avoidance. Troy laughed that I was moving slowly but I think he was a little hungover as well.

Troy's dad is a police officer and during the drive to Playa Tamarindo we happened upon him, sitting on the side of the road with his radar gun. Troy pulled over to introduce us and they talked briefly before we got back to our excursion over mostly dirt roads. It was nice to be welcomed back to Capitan Suizo, even if it was just for one night. I immediately called Nati to tell her we had arrived and we made plans to meet up.

Troy wanted to watch a futbol game and since the hotel rooms didn't have televisions he talked one of the staff members into letting him watch the game at the staff residence while I reconnected with Nati for a drink (nothing cures a hangover like another drink), beach walk and a chat.
On our stroll we found Sophie and Alice playing in the trees. Nati also pointed out the hotel's newest family member, a baby named Maggie. Just a few months old, she was found by a local resident who brought her to the hotel to be cared for after suffering a head injury. She was blind in one eye and I was glad that she had caretakers to support her.

Later, Troy and I watched an incredible sunset before meeting up with Nati for dinner at a local restaurant where her friend, Avelino, was singing. The food was awful, we all agreed, but the environment was nice: open air on the beach, good music, and good friends. Avelino was from Brazil and one of the reasons I like Tamarindo so much is because it's a melting pot. While many of the tourists are from the United States, the residents of the town are actually from all over the world which I feel creates an interesting vibe .

Troy and I were going to meet Avelino at another bar after his set but were too tired from so much traveling. We decided to return to the hotel and relax on the patio chairs outside our bungalow. We drank a few beers but didn't say much to one another. Things were still awkward between us and I couldn't help but wonder if Troy was keeping me at arms distance...knowing I would be going home again not wanting to make parting worse by getting too close.

The next morning, Troy and I enjoyed our breakfast as we watched the local magpies try to steal people's food (ours, included).

We took one last walk on the beach and then packed up our things to head out of town. Even though our time together didn't turn out the way I would have liked, I was still sad to see it coming to an end. I knew that in just two short hours, we would be arriving back at his mom's house and we'd be saying goodbye to each other, once again. Road work slowed the drive, prolonging the inevitable.

I was quiet on the ride and Troy tried to engage me, asking me if I was okay. Though there were many things I could have said in that moment, I just admitted that I was sad my trip was now over. He leaned over indicating he wanted a kiss, his way of letting me know we would be okay. We pulled up to his mom's house and said our goodbyes. I climbed into the driver's side but he pulled me towards him to give me one last embrace. The light affection was confusing to me, given his prohibition of our sex life. As I made a u-turn, I could see in my rear view mirror Troy walking toward his house but he turned at one point to give a quick wave goodbye. I brought my hand up to acknowledge him with a twinge of bittersweet emotion. The situation would be much easier to wrap my head around if we had just parted ways... hugs, kisses and turning around to watch me leave, those things to me hinted at a greater level of intimacy that he was no longer willing to share.

Back in San Jose, I had an appointment to meet with a design firm, Into-Designs, that afternoon. They had done the design work for several of the hotels I'd stayed with and I liked their work. I wanted to meet with them about designing my first book. Since driving in San Jose (even with a GPS) is challenging, Silvia met me halfway at a hospital which was easy to locate and then I followed the rest of the way to her office.

Silvia and Maureen made me feel so welcome and even offered me a sweet gift, a journal made from lemon paper. I selected their firm to design the business card for my photography company since they were out of my price range for the book design work. I also hired them to design the cover of this book and I hope to work with them again in the future.

Looking back on this trip, I'm very pleased with everything I got to do and see. Not everything went as I had hoped it would but then again, this is life and life is imperfect and always changing, producing new and beautiful endeavors if we choose to recognize them. I choose not to dwell on the sad events (and trust me, I could have written a lot more about the disagreement between Troy and I) but instead to delight in the joyful moments; the moments where there was laughter and love, harmony and peace. I'm certain that this brings me more freedom than the other option.

## Chapter 11

*Ocotal-Rincon de la Vieja-Tamarindo*

November 2009

I had a redeye flight, headed to Miami on my way to Costa Rica. Once on the plane, I grabbed my pillow (side note: American's pillows are larger than Delta), took two Tylenol PM tablets and tried to fall asleep. Luckily, take off put me to sleep and I was sleepily content until the flight attendant began speaking on the intercom, asking if there was a physician on board. I slowly opened my eyes and saw that she looked terrified. I couldn't see anything because they drew the curtain but we didn't have to complete an emergency landing so I reasoned that everything was working out ok. I tried to go back to sleep but the passenger next to me started snoring. I'm sure he didn't appreciate me opening the window at 4 a.m. but if I were able to sleep, perhaps I wouldn't have done it. The current time was 7 a.m. so it wasn't all that early.

I made my way to the Admirals Club, got some coffee and breakfast, found the showers and instantly, I felt refreshed.

The woman who checked me in gave me a drink ticket, so I found my way to the bar, ordered a mimosa and waited for my connecting flight. Having a three hour layover is never desirable but it's made worthwhile when I get to use the Admirals Club for free.

The second leg of my trip wasn't so bad. The passenger next to me was originally from Argentina, visiting Costa Rica for the first time. I recommended a few restaurants and activities to check out in the cities he would be visiting, happy to share my extensive almost Tica knowledge. As usual, there were no vegetarian options for lunch, but the flight attendant was willing to work with me, removing the filet mignon before heating the meal. The starter salad was good and the veggies (sans carne) were okay. It was better than nothing but I was still frustrated that a dead animal was my plate just moments before it was brought to me.

A representative from Dollar Rent-a-Car was actually waiting for me at the airport when I arrived, a refreshing change of pace from some of my other trips. They offered me their new Nissan SUV, kind of like a Xterra, maybe a little smaller. The roads to Ocotal weren't so bad; other than the fifty or so potholes which looked like small sinkholes. The GPS even worked (almost) perfectly. It directed me to continue going straight which would have landed me in the Pacific Ocean but somehow I found my way to the left turn that led me to my hotel.

The hotel was nice, not as nice as other places I've stayed (I've become a little spoiled with the Cayuga managed properties), but I decided it would do, especially when I remembered Troy's opinion that I was a hotel snob. The room had separate living and bedroom areas, which was a plus but the true bonus was that my room was just steps from the beach. I doubted that I would hear any monkeys but there were lots of birds and iguanas.

The iguanas I could see from my room reminded me of the one crossing the road on my drive. He wouldn't get out of the road, which was only one lane so I couldn't try to go around. He was definitely on Tico time and seeming to try and communicate with me that I'd be so much happier if I'd just join him in that endeavor.

I settled in with a late lunch at the pool and reacquainted myself with a few Bavaria Golds.

I took a deep breath…and suddenly life was good again.

I woke up early the next morning and took a walk on the beach. It was a great morning for photography, the shadows and sunlight gave off interesting reflections and golden glimmers. The tide was out and the tide pools were filled with little fish and other sea life. There was a beautiful King Heron looking for its breakfast. I took a few moments to watch the crabs scurry around, making sand art.

At breakfast, just like in Tamarindo, the magpies were out, attempting to abscond with food items belonging to less than vigilant vacationers. They were very assertive in their lurking, and two tried to storm my table as I was looking off to the ocean. They scooted a few feet away once they knew they had been seen but another table wasn't so lucky. At that table, a magpie tipped over a little tray of Splenda and ended up with about eight packets in his mouth. I fervently hoped that he didn't eat them as he flew away with the packets before anyone could retrieve them. I feared for his digestion but I was amused by their persistence.

Later that night, as I walked toward the restaurant, I noticed a raccoon trying to get inside. He tried the glass doors first, but found them closed. Next he waddled up an embankment of rocks which led to the windows of the restaurant; some of which were open. Peering inside he appeared to be weighing his options. In the end he decided to waddle off, presumably to find an easier meal elsewhere. I chuckled to think of how I would have responded if I had looked up from my dinner to find myself face to face with a raccoon contemplating stealing away my veggies. Animal table companions were just something I had come to expect for all of my meals in Costa Rica.

I took a trip to a brand new shopping center, which looked out of place in the old town of Coco. The market, AutoMercado was probably one of the nicest I've been in and was fully stocked with everything I could possibly need. I was surprised to see that they had a lot of the type of groceries I've come to expect from large State-side grocers like Whole Foods.

Domestic beer ran about $1.35/bottle which seemed high. When I got the bottles back to the hotel, I stuck them in the mini-fridge but when I went to re-open the door, the bottles rolled out. The first escaped bottle rolled out and broke all over the bedroom floor. Sadly, the comedy of errors continued. As I was dealing with the broken bottle, two more rolled out. Fortunately, only one of those broke, but the bedroom did reek of beer for the next day or so.

Troy and I were still trying to coordinate our schedules and when we would see each other. He had just been offered a position with the government and had to take care of paperwork in San Jose which made it not so convenient for us to see each other.

We finally figured out when we could meet up and he took a bus to Liberia and I picked him up at the shopping center. I was so excited when I pulled into the center and saw him there, waiting for me. I stopped the car in the middle of the parking lot, jumped out and gave him a huge hug, all the while stopping the traffic behind us. Troy had wanted to drive but I needed to put him on the insurance and didn't want him to pull into the car rental agency driving the vehicle (I'm very conservative when it comes to legal issues such as this). So we worked out the vehicle situation and then he drove us back to the hotel. I warned him about the potholes and he just laughed. We stopped at the market to pick up a few more beers (since I had broken the ones I had bought earlier in the week) and food.

Later, we visited Playa Hermosa which truly was a beautiful beach (hermosa means beautiful in Spanish). As usual, Troy knew someone there and he managed to get us access to the lounge chairs at the beach which belonged to a local, private community.

The temperature of the water was perfect. Sadly, I found a plastic ring (for a 6 pack of soda/beer) floating in the water which I took out and handed to Troy who tore the rings apart and gave it to a local vendor to throw away. It's such a detriment to the sea life and birds and so heartbreaking to see in this otherwise pristine location.

After spending a few hours in the sun at Hermosa, Troy had asked another friend where the best location was to view the sunset since, in Ocotal, there is a mountain to the west, blocking most of the sunset over the ocean. His friend recommended Costa Blanca which is a hotel however you can tell the guard at the gate you're going to the cliffs to watch the sunset and they'll let you through. While this was private property, all of the beaches in Costa Rica are considered public and the private land owners must allow open access. There were hundreds of dragonflies on this cliff and while there were very few clouds (which make for a better photo at sunset), it was still so beautiful to watch. We also met a fun group of people while we were there. Although when we pulled out our beers, they seemed upset we didn't have enough for all of them.

The next morning, we had a quick breakfast before taking off for Rincon de la Vieja National Park. It's about a seventy-five minute drive from Ocotal and I will definitely visit this park again. Guanacaste is an interesting region of Costa Rica. It's considered dry (but still humid) and almost desert-like. While hiking through the Park, we not only came across areas of desert fields but also rainforest areas, both of which had different plant and animal life. Rincon de la Vieja is a volcano but isn't considered active.

However, a few weeks before my trip I had read they had closed the Park as they were concerned about volcanic activity. I also read that while the volcano is still kind of active, they don't generally worry about explosions because of the activity with the mud pots. Basically, the volcano is letting off steam in the surrounding area so it doesn't need to have an active lava flow like Arenal. I was excited to see what a "mud pot" was!

On our hike, we passed by large ant hills (about four feet high by five feet wide), we saw a "volcanito" (small volcanic crater) and several areas of fumaroles (mud pots) with temperatures around 200 degrees. While it was an unpleasant odor (imagine the smell of sulfa which is similar to a rotting egg smell), it was really fun to watch the bubbling mud.

The hike we selected also had a beautiful waterfall; probably the best one I've seen thus far. Unfortunately, trying to get a photo was somewhat challenging and while I was trying to focus on not falling on the slippery rocks, I completely forgot to get a panoramic photo (like I said, I'll have to go back).

It should be mentioned here that Troy and I got back together again prior to my arrival in Ocotal. I don't know what changed his mind after our argument in Osa and I decided it was best not to ask. I was just happy to have him in my life again. While we did have a few nice days together, it was much too short and I was disappointed when Troy returned from an errand to tell me he wouldn't be joining me in Tamarindo for the weekend. I understood he needed to prepare to move for his job and there were other things like paperwork that needed to be handled but I was still saddened. I don't know why I think anything different will happen but I choose to live an optimist's life and am forever hopeful. Troy drove us back to the main intersection which would take him home (in one direction) and me to Tamarindo (in the opposite direction). He got out of the car and we did our usual goodbyes. As I drove away, I could see him turn around as he walked away, waving his hand goodbye.

Tamarindo was a whirlwind of a trip. Arriving at noon on a Friday, I had lunch and then Nati came to the hotel looking for me. I caught up with her for a few hours, drinking a few beers at the bar. That night, I went on a turtle watching tour for green turtles and met a very nice family from Cardiff by the Sea which is near San Diego, California. Laura turned out to be a travel photographer and had some amazing equipment with her. For the night shoot, she had a special (and very heavy) lens that would allow her to take photos without a flash since we can't shoot the turtles with flash and the tour is done in the dark. I was impressed as she was carrying not only the camera body, but also the large lens and a tripod. That's why I like my Sony point and shoot and don't want to invest in a DSLR. While DSLR's may take sharper photos, they require way too much equipment.

The tour, I was told, would be an easy fifteen minute walk on the beach. So, I figured I'd just wear my ked sandals. Well, as it turns out, it wasn't an easy fifteen minute walk on the beach. When we arrived at the first beach, there weren't any turtles (and we were told at that point there normally aren't on this beach) so we had to hike up a mountain with steep, rocky terrain (about thirty meters) and then, of course, hike back down the other side of the mountain to get to the beach. But it was well worth it since we saw three green turtles...one that had hatched her eggs and was heading back to the ocean and two that were building their nests and then laying their eggs.

It was a National Geographic moment to watch the eggs pop out of the turtles! There were about 120 eggs laid between the two turtles. The turtles slowly create an enormous hole with their back flippers (about two feet deep) to lay their eggs. Once they are done, they cover the hole up and head back to the ocean. However, because of poaching, the guides grabbed the eggs before they were buried and put them in a plastic bag for the first one and then in a t-shirt of one of the guides for the second turtle (they didn't bring enough plastic bags). Then, our guides went to another spot on the beach and dug holes which were two feet deep and replanted the eggs. Our guides had to relocate them to an area where there weren't turtle trails in the sand because the poachers arrive in the early morning, see the trails made by the turtles and dig up the eggs. We were told they are a delicacy but I can't understand why it would be any different than a chicken egg. Turtles are endangered and I find it very sad these extra steps have to be taken to protect them. I also wonder what the mom is thinking with us standing there, grabbing her eggs. I hope she knows we are only trying to help.

On Saturday, the same family from the turtle tour joined me on a snorkeling tour. And again, Laura had an amazing underwater lens which had been custom made. Our guide, Santiago, took my underwater camera a few times to get shots of the fish that I didn't want to go near, like the barracuda and eel. Plus, he can dive much deeper than me. I just kind of like to float on the surface and if I see something really interesting, then I'll dive down. He found a puffer fish and some very pretty starfish. I touched the puffer fish and Ouch! I couldn't believe he was holding it; its little spikes were incredibly painful. ***Which I will just note here that I don't condone touching animals. I think Santiago's good looks were distracting me from my values. ***

We snorkeled in two locations just outside of Tamarindo and on both sites I was stung by invisible jellyfish. At first, it was just my left wrist so while it painful and became red and bumpy, I was thankful it wasn't on my shooting hand. But at the second site, they attacked my right hand and it was then that I called it a day. Santiago did pour something, possibly ammonia, on it and we all joked about it being urine. We also saw a few dolphins, two green turtles mating and poisonous sea snakes.

Later, I went to lunch with the family (I was invited by Zuri, their 7 year old daughter) and I learned more about their travels. They were headed down to Lapa Rios and then Arenas del Mar and while they had already been to Lapa Rios, I gave them some tips for Arenas del Mar. They are a vegetarian family so we talked about how it can be difficult to get vegetarian meals while traveling. The EcoLodges, however, generally do have more vegetarian meals available. And none of us had any complaints about the food at Lapa Rios or the selection. Troy and I both agree we would go back there again, just to experience the food!

That afternoon, Santiago met me at Capitan Suizo. He was going to teach me how to surf but the tide was out and the conditions just weren't amenable so we decided to visit his hometown of Santa Rosa, which is about 10km outside of Tamarindo. He didn't know much English which made things a little more interesting. However, I have to say I was so impressed with my Spanish abilities. I guess when I'm put on the spot, I really do know more than I think I do! We played a few rounds of pool which was so much fun since I haven't played in years. There were a few times when I sank a ball into the pocket on a really hard shot and Santiago would look at me, wondering if I was some kind of hustler!

Later, we went to the town's rodeo. I think it was my karma for attending the rodeo because this is when I was attacked by the bugs. For this trip, I tried out natural Vitamin B1 patches which were supposed to keep the bugs at bay (and they don't smell like the Burt's Bees) but let me tell you, they definitely don't work. I was attacked in Santa Rosa and my feet were covered in huge red, itchy, painful bumps. I tried pouring tea tree oil on them but it didn't seem to help.

The rodeo started out with cowboys riding their horses which was nice and non-violent. However, when they brought the bulls in, my heart just sank. I understand this is a part of the traditional Tico culture and history and it's very important to them but it's also just so heartbreaking. Not just the bull riding itself but everything leading up to it and then after the rider has fallen off and they have to try to round up the bull. There was this sad, frightened look on this little bull's face that I cannot get out of my head. He had three lassoes around his neck and they were pulling him and forcing him in different directions. It was just awful. And that's when I told Santiago it was time for me to go back to the hotel. I appreciate the cultural experience but it's not something I would do again.

I had a very sweet, but short, encounter with the babies at Capitan Suizo. Two of whom can no longer be considered babies. When I look back at the photo of me and Sophie from eighteen months ago, I can't believe how big she's gotten! As well as healthy and strong. Alice is also full size now and many times, I found her quietly playing in the trees by my bungalow. Little Maggie has also doubled in size and I caught some video of her and Sophie roughhousing in the trees. However, while they may play rough at times, Sophie is also highly protective of her "sister". One night, they were sitting on the roof of one of the bungalows when a family of raccoons showed up and Sophie let the raccoons know they were not welcome.

Sadly, there is now a new addition, Lola. Only three or four months old, Lola was found on the beach with her mom (remember howlers almost never come down from the canopies of the trees). Both were very malnourished and looked like they had been abused. They were brought to the hotel by a local resident but Lola's mom didn't make it. She was probably trying to put so much energy into caring for her child that she became malnourished herself. Lola is still very small but an active little girl. She is also very much attached to her caretaker (who, with nonverbal communication, makes it very clear we are not to approach her little ones). Nati continues to provide me with updates on the monkeys and tells me Lola is growing and getting healthier. It also appears she has been accepted by Sophie, Alice and Maggie. Like Maggie, Lola had an injury and is also blind in one eye.

Like Maggie, Lola had an injury and is also blind in one eye.

## Chapter 12

*Nosara-Punta Islita-Canas-Papagayo*

I took a detour before going to Punta Islita to visit Sibu Sanctuary in Nosara. I'd had several communications with Steve and Vicki Coan, the founders, who were a part of Nosara Wildlife, a nonprofit organization dedicated to helping injured and orphaned monkeys and other animals. I was excited to meet them and see their sanctuary. They were so welcoming and kind. They worked tirelessly to care for, and protect, the animals in their care. They were also actively involved in education and outreach, areas in which I found myself gaining interest.

One of the main issues in the area, and the country for that matter, was the electrical lines being installed without insulation in the rural areas. Vicki told stories of monkeys she had personally witnessed and it brought tears to my eyes thinking about the tragic deaths of innocent animals, which could have been prevented. She told me the monkeys scream in pain, unable to let go of the wire and when they finally can, their burned bodies fall to the ground and most of them die.

Many times, members of the troop heard the screams and tried to help... only to be electrocuted themselves. It is estimated that in the last 12 years, over 50% of the Costa Rican monkey population has died with one of top reasons cited as the electrical lines installed due to the massive development occurring in remote areas of the jungles and near the beaches.

Vicki let me into the secure habitat area, where most visitors aren't allowed, and I was able to see the monkeys, that were being rehabilitated, up close. They were so playful and sweet, although they would sometimes try to give little bites or pull on my hair. The Harmony Hotel, where I stayed on my second trip, donated the construction materials for their habitat but it was clear that much more work (and funding) would be needed.

The sanctuary also had orphaned baby squirrels, which they were caring for, as well as a raccoon and her babies. It was such a pleasure meeting Steve and Vicki. I could tell that while it was very challenging work, this was their true calling and they felt just as blessed as the animals they cared for to be part of the solution.

I had planned to stop by the beach in Nosara and take a few moments to reminisce about my first visit there and meeting Troy, but I decided to skip it this time around. The memories were still so vivid in my heart; I didn't need to take the time to see the location.

I was glad that I hadn't taken the extra time when it took me about 4 times as long to get to my next hotel as I'd expected. My travels became difficult when I was just six kilometers away and the GPS was telling me to turn left and traverse a river.

There hadn't been much rain so I figured that it was worth a shot but I couldn't find the road that would even let me get to the river, much less cross it. I ended up at someone's private property which was a dead end.

I called the hotel for guidance and they advised me to take the principal road (since I didn't have 4WD in the X-Trail) to Santa Marta. A sign ahead of me indicated Santa Marta with a left arrow next to it. Logically, I assumed that meant to turn left onto the dirt road across from the sign but was puzzled as it led in the opposite direction of the river. As it turned out, the dirt road went nowhere and apparently I was meant to go straight, despite the arrow. With a frustrated groan, I navigated back onto the main road and shortly thereafter saw a sign that said Punta Islita: Twelve kilometers. I breathed a sigh of relief and assured myself that I had only had 20 more minutes on the road.

Over an hour later, I finally arrived at the hotel. I didn't get lost again; the road was just adventurous. After a couple steep and winding hills (a few of which were unpaved) I crashed into one major ditch but I only came close to spinning the tires twice. Fortunately, having just been at Sibu where I stalled on their hill I had learned that you just had to floor the gas going up the hill and not worry about the rocks and ditches (or you would't make it).

Security let me through the Punta Islita gate and Leonardo, one of the concierges, greeted me in the parking lot. He handed me a cool, wet towel, which was desperately needed after gripping the steering wheel and sweating (with the a/c on) for an hour. He also offered me a welcome drink and while I thought he probably meant a smoothie or soda, I asked for a cerveza. I deserved it.

Punta Islita sat atop a hill overlooking the Pacific and was very remote - not as remote as Lapa Rios - but close. The bungalows all had private terraces with views and hammocks. I got settled into my room but I wasn't able to get the internet to work which wouldn't have fazed me if I was only traveling for fun but since I had work to do I called the concierge. After about an hour of troubleshooting, they ended up moving me to a room closer to the reception desk where the adapter was located. It turned out that the room they moved me to was the honeymoon suite and it came with a private jacuzzi, hammock and lounge chairs and of course, it overlooked the ocean and jungle. Even the bathroom was well appointed and beautiful.

After such a long day, I really just wanted to veg out and thought about ordering room service but was disappointed with the limited vegetarian options available. I called the restaurant to ask if they could provide me with additional options and the server had the chef call me back directly, pleased to offer stuffed eggplant, Portobello, risotto with mushrooms or vegetable fajitas. It was so nice to visit a place willing to go above and beyond. They took excellent care of me.

The next morning, I was woken up by the sound of Parakeets. They had eluded me the week before when I was in Ocotal but finally, they were in a tree close enough to photograph them. There were about fifteen birds in the tree, singing their morning song, quite loudly, as the sun rose over the mountain.

A few months before my trip, I learned that my body had been reacting to several different things such as gluten, alcohol and sugar and I'd placed myself on a limited diet, however while on vacation, I had no real desire to be so restrictive. Tico food was actually pretty good for me (with the exception of the beer) and I knew it was unrealistic to expect perfection, especially when I wasn't able to prepare all of my own meals. When the hotel staff brought me a homemade birthday cake to my room, I was incredibly touched by their thoughtfulness. There was no way I was going to be rude and refuse their lovely gesture, despite the fact that so much sugar would inevitably require a raw food cleanse upon my return to the States. I decided to have my cake and eat it too... and it was deliciously worth it.

After a week of go-go-go, I decided to take a day to just do nothing. I did venture into town but Punta Islita is very small and basically consists of a small museum and community center in which many housewives were meeting to make crafts for the souvenir shop. The town boasted a school, futbol field (of course), a church that had bats hanging from the rafters (the doors were open this time, at least), a sacred forest which I would still like to learn more about and a pulperia. A pulperia is a very, very small market, similar to a 7-11 but smaller and with a few more staple food items. It you blinked you could easily miss it but it was quaint and exploring it made for a perfect down time day.

Later that afternoon, I was lying in the hammock when I started to hear a tell-tale sign of monkeys nearby... the sound of breaking branches. A few feet away from me there was an entire troop of howler monkeys. The adults seemed to be sleeping but the babies were playing. Eventually though, naptime ended and everyone started traversing the branches, looking for good leaves to eat. I felt so truly blessed to share space with those beautiful animals. It was fascinating to watch them interact and carry out their daily existence, live and in person. Watching shows on National Geographic has nothing on seeing them eat, sleep, and play firsthand.

The next morning, I learned of a hiking trail on the property and set off to explore the jungle alone. It was nice to have some solitary time out there; listening to the sounds of the stream below me, the birds' overhead and the monkeys in the distance. The canopy of the trees provided me with relief from the hot sun and I took my time wandering down the path, looking at the pretty flowers, the interesting fungi growing off the bark of trees and the morphos who were hiding their beautiful blue color from me and trying to blend into the tree trunk where they were resting.

While there were so many things to see and hear in the jungle, I also found a quiet, meditative peacefulness being in that place. It was marvelous to be away from the sounds of cars and construction. Though Sonoma County is relatively quiet, compared to a big city like San Francisco or Los Angeles, there is a much deeper sense of calm and quiet in the jungle that speaks to me in a way that California never could.

After the hike, I walked down to the hotel's private beach and sat for a few moments on a lounge chair. Still in a meditative mood, I was contemplating my time there on the Rich Coast. I felt fortunate to have the time, money and resources to be able to see all that I had seen. I thought about how much I would love to make the move to Costa Rica and live there permanently as I walked along the beach. The overwhelming sense of peace I felt there told me that it was only a matter of time.

It started to rain after my walk and kept up through the following morning. I have to admit I was a little concerned about my drive down the unpaved mountain. I hoped that I wouldn't get stuck in the mud but then remembered that the dirt roads in Costa Rica dried out much quicker than back home and I probably didn't have to worry. If only. I refer to that drive as my personal version of Mr. Toad's Wild Ride from Disneyland... I got incredibly lost getting down the mountain. The GPS tried to direct me to cross the river (again) and for whatever reason I wasn't able to retrace my original steps, so it took me about an hour to find the principal road.

Unfortunately, as I started an incline the paved road became dirt, with more than its fair share of potholes. The most unfortunate part about the potholes was that I couldn't always see the depth, resulting in a lot of jolts, bumps and shakes. There were also no homes or cities in sight and very few cars or people passing by on my jarring excursion. The rain picked up just as my GPS just stopped working. I was also starting to run low on gas. I eventually arrived in a town called Hojancha and found a school where a nice young man helped me find my way back to the main road the old fashioned way - using a map, which thankfully I had in the car - and directed me to a gas station.

About fifteen minutes later, the road became familiar again and I sensed I was on the road Troy and I had taken to

Tamarindo during the last trip. I passed over the Tempisque River Bridge and began to feel a little more relaxed. The GPS still wasn't working so when I saw a police officer on the side of the road waiting for speeders, I pulled over to see if he could help me find the way to my next stop, Las Pumas Animal Sanctuary. As it turned out, the police officer was Troy's dad again but since he didn't speak English, it made things a little more difficult. He finally understood that I wanted directions and he was able to help. He had a friend with him, who needed a ride to Cañas. I'm not one to pick up hitchhikers but since she was with Troy's dad, I figured it would be okay. She didn't speak English either but we conversed a bit with my minimal Spanish.

I was excited to visit Las Pumas as both Troy and Nati had mentioned it to me. Nati had painted a beautiful piece of the jaguar that resided at the property. The shelter cared for five of the six varieties of big cats indigenous to Costa Rica and were either becoming or are already considered endangered: ocelots, margay's, jaguarundi's, pumas and jaguars. They also rehabilitated many other animals that had been hunted or injured, including foxes, raccoons, monkeys, otters and birds. Founded over forty years before by the late Lilly Bodmer de Hagunauer, the shelter received no government funding, but still managed to care for about eighty animals and twenty-two different species. I was so grateful for their work, rescuing animals that had endured so much before coming to them.

After my visit to the shelter, I drove to my final destination on the Papagayo Peninsula. I was completely exhausted from the last two weeks of travel and decided to take the afternoon to relax and read on the deck of my room, which overlooked the beautiful green bay.

It was hard to focus on my book though as thoughts of Troy came to mind. Our relationship often wasn't what I hoped it would be but I wondered if it wasn't still somehow exactly what it needed to be. I also thought about the fact that my third trip in a year was at its end. It went by much too quickly but I was also content with all that I had experienced. I felt blessed to have had the opportunity to visit so frequently, though of course when you're visiting your love, 3 times in a year doesn't feel frequent. I felt a tingle of anticipation for what the future would bring even as I dealt with the dreaded task of packing to leave.

The next morning during check out I paid the departure tax at the hotel which was a lovely perk since standing at the airport with all of your luggage, trying to fill out forms can feel a bit overwhelming. My flight ended up being delayed so I purchased my last Bavaria Gold and enjoyed the final few moments of humid air while waiting in the open-air airport. On the approach to Miami Airport, there was a spectacular sunset taking place and I decided to photograph the skyline.

The flight attendant asked me to put away my camera, as I wasn't allowed to use it during the flight. I knew full well that the actual prohibition was on cameras with wireless capabilities and which my Sony didn't have. While I do my best to follow rules and be respectful, I still snuck in a few shots when he wasn't looking because I knew that I wouldn't be causing any trouble with the flight.

Arriving in Miami on Thanksgiving Day was one of my best travel choices. There was hardly anyone on the plane and arriving back in Miami, I sailed through customs and immigration as well as the security checkpoint to get back into the terminal for my connecting flight.

On the flight to San Francisco I got to experience the fully reclining seats, which basically transform into a small bed. Preflight snacks consisted of warm nuts and a cold Heineken, followed by an exceptional three course vegetarian dinner with wine and cookies and ice cream sundaes for dessert. Once completely satiated, I reclined the seat, curled up with the provided blanket and pillow and took a little nap. Afterward, I watched a movie on the personal DVD player the flight attendant had handed out, prior to take-off. I was in such a blissful state; fully convinced that this was really the only way to fly, especially since I was headed back to a home that didn't feel like home anymore.

It was on the flight to San Francisco that I first experienced the fully reclining seats which basically transform into a small bed. Preflight snacks consisted of warm nuts and a cold Heineken.

This was followed by an exceptional three course vegetarian dinner with wine and cookies and ice cream sundaes for dessert. Once completely satiated, I reclined the seat fully, curled up with the provided blanket and pillow and took a little nap which was followed by watching a movie on the personal DVD player the flight attendant had handed out, prior to take-off. I was in such a blissful state; this was really the only way to fly.

# Chapter 13

Jicaro Island-Granada, Nicaragua

January 2010

During my time back in the states, I started to have some serious health problems requiring MRI tests and trips to the neurologist. It was scary to feel like I wasn't healthy and in control of my body. Thankfully, Troy and I after some time incommunicado were able to reconnect. He was very emotionally supportive and a great friend through all of my health concerns. I realized how much I missed him and how good he could be for me after a brief relationship with a charming but manipulative man back in the States. We might not be destined to ride off into the sunset together but at least I knew he wasn't just trying to get a free international trip out of me or steal my personal and intellectual property.

Between the health issues, stress from having so many ongoing projects and the fact that California no longer felt like home, I was more than ready to go back again, although this time I intended to see Nicaragua. Many people in my life, remembering how volatile and war torn Nicaragua had been several years before, questioned why I didn't visit New Zealand or Hawaii but the truth is my heart belonged to Central America.

May 2010

It was a beautiful day to fly into Miami. There were very few clouds, the sun had just risen and the Miami skyline was featured in an incredible light. With a three-hour layover, I made my way to the Admirals Club, as a nice hot shower and cup of coffee were what I needed after a long red eye. I looked up at the display screen and saw that it was 8:00 a.m. in Nicaragua and already 80 degrees. I couldn't wait to arrive and feel the warm sun and humid air. It had been a very long and cold El Niño winter in Northern California, with morning temperatures still in the 30s, which was generally unheard of and difficult for my body to tolerate. My body, mind and spirit desperately needed the warm sunshine, the embrace of mi amor and a new country for my inner Pippy to explore.

Nicaragua is a part of the Pacific Ring of Fire, an area of the Pacific prone to earthquakes and volcanoes. Nicaragua has over forty-five volcanoes of which almost half are active. There are even two volcanoes on Omotepe Island on Lake Nicaragua and people still live on the islands at the base of the volcanoes.

The country was taken over by Spain in 1524, has some interesting historical tales of problems with pirates in colonial times and sadly most of the indigenous culture has disappeared. They have a lot of dry forest, which means that in the dry season, the trees lose their leaves and much of the landscape is brown unlike the lushness of Costa Rica's rainforests. In addition to earthquakes they are also in the hurricane zone. While I didn't visit their beaches, I was told they are beautiful and there are some incredible surf spots, with waves reaching over twenty feet. Much of the country is jungles and farms with only a few main cities such as Granada, Masaya, Managua and Leon. Something I appreciated greatly compared to my travels in Costa Rica was that the principal roads were all nicely paved and well maintained.

The average monthly income of a schoolteacher is about $200 US dollars. Catholicism is the main religion though with a greater focus on the Virgin Mary. In the Granada cathedral, there was a statue of Mary at the altar instead of a cross with Jesus. Because of US influence, baseball is the major pastime outranking even futbol.

Nicaragua had its share of insects, just as in Costa Rica. However, I didn't get any bug bites while I was there and while the chayules flies were somewhat bothersome at times (they kept landing in my glass of wine), I also recognized their importance to the lake's ecosystem.

The airport in Nicaragua was actually much more efficient than I imagined it would be. Flying first class, I got through immigration and customs quickly because I was one of the first off the plane. The hotel had hired a driver for me and I could see him waiting on the outside with a sign that said my name. I have to admit I was concerned they would forget to pick me up. Ever since the first rental car incident, I continued to fear being stuck at the airport.

My driver was so very kind though. He spoke a little English and talked with me about his country on the hour long drive to the boat dock. We passed a fruit stand on our way and he stopped the car and bought me two mangoes excited to share them with me. He pointed out each of the volcanoes we drove past and told me we were on the Pan-American Highway which ran between both North and South America. It was amusing to think about the thoroughfare we were on being a major roadway as as we were driving past horse drawn carriages and people on bicycles, but I respectfully stifled a giggle.

Later, Troy told me that Nicaragua was about twenty years behind Costa Rica. His statement was so very true. It's a different world from Costa Rica but of course, it also has its similarities. I found the people to be very friendly and respectful. I never felt unsafe, even when we drove through poverty stricken areas. With the exception of the military base we passed which was near the border of Costa Rica, I don't think I saw a single police officer.

When we arrived at the boat dock, I was greeted by Carolina who had a huge smile on her face. She walked me to the boat on which I'd take a ten-minute ride to Jicaro Island Ecolodge, one of over 300 islands on Lake Nicaragua. Despite the standard pronunciation of vowels in Spanish, the name of the island is pronounced hick-a-row, which I learned from Troy over the phone. I kept calling it he-car-oh and Troy had no idea what I was talking about until I spelled it for him. He couldn't pass up the opportunity to razz me for my poor Spanish-speaking skills, even though in this case, it was the island breaking the rules, not me. He liked to joke with me that he was only going to speak to me in Spanish. We tried that a few times but he talked too fast and we both got frustrated.

The boat ride to Jicaro Island was just beautiful. My driver didn't seem to speak English but I was okay with just enjoying the scenery and breathing in the fresh air. We passed numerous shore birds such as cormorants and egrets, sitting on rocks, waiting for their dinner of fish to appear. Lily pads and other lake plant life were prevalent throughout the maze of islands as well.

Our boat drove parallel to Mombacho Volcano and it looked like an immense mountain, covered in trees and cloudy at the top. Navigating took quite a bit of effort and knowledge of the lake since there were so many different routes and water levels could change causing damage to the underside of boat. I was told there were over 300 islands. Many of them were too small for inhabitants, though just one family called some home. Ometepe on the other hand had two active volcanoes and numerous residents. Passing by the smaller islands gave me a little glimpse into the lives of the residents there. They hung clothes to dry on their clotheslines while kids ran around playing tag. I couldn't imagine living on a tiny island but the day-to-day tasks looked familiar and comforting. I also saw quite a few chicken coops and supposed that many of these residents lived off the land and probably didn't go into Granada very often.

Claudia was the first to welcome me to the Jicaro. She was seven months pregnant and truly radiant, handing me a glass of iced tea with a reusable bamboo straw. She told me the tea was made from a local grass. It was so delicious and refreshing in the hot afternoon sun.

Jicaro had an open-air kitchen and restaurant where you could talk to and get to know the chefs and kitchen staff while watching them prepare your meal. The restaurant served traditional Nicaraguan meals with a modern, gourmet twist and large portion sizes. It was delectable and I highly recommend the gallo pinto "burger". I was also extremely impressed that they remembered I had informed them that I was a vegetarian through email six months before.

My first meal there was just a light serving of homemade hummus with veggies and pita slices accompanied by fresh Tamarindo juice. While it wasn't anything out of the ordinary, I was so pleased to be able to have real Tamarindo juice again.

The ecolodge also had spa treatment rooms, a yoga deck, and a cenote, a circular structure with different levels and water in the center, almost like a tiered labyrinth. It was the perfect place for contemplation and meditation. While there were many off island adventures to participate in, I could just as easily stay on the island and be perfectly content; taking a siesta in a hammock, enjoying the 360° views at the Mirador, lounging by the pool or kayaking around the lake.

*Sustainability at Jicaro*

On my first night at Jicaro, I was given a tour of the lodge's sustainability practices, from the ground up, by Matt (or Mateo as the Jicaro staff call him). Matt was from California but had been living in Nicaragua for the last decade, first as a Peace Corps worker and then as a consultant for Jicaro during its construction and opening.

I learned the wood, which was used to build the nine casitas and common areas, was either FSC certified, RAN certified or reclaimed. Much of it came from Hurricane Felix in 2007. The stones and the rocks that made up the pathways were from the island and they left all of the trees in their original locations, building the casitas around them.

The hotel actively educated the staff on sustainability issues such as composting and recycling and they provided the staff with healthy meals during their shifts. They had a water filtration system, making it possible to drink the tap water so we did not have to use plastic, non-reusable bottles. They used local organic food and worked with local farmers and bakers. They provided signs in the rooms and in the "back of the house" for reminders about lights, fans, water and other resources that both guests and staff used on a daily basis. The materials in the rooms were organic and almost everything came from local companies in Nicaragua.

Matt and Chef Calley were the only employees on staff that weren't local to Nicaragua. They each had short-term contracts to provide guidance during the opening of the hotel but in the future, all employees will be from the local area, which, in turn, supports the local economy. I was pleased to see firsthand that Cayuga had outshone my expectations once again.

Claudia's husband, Fabian, was the Sustainability Director for Jicaro and my guide for most of the tours I did in Nicaragua. Our first was a walking tour of Granada. I was so impressed with Fabian's knowledge of both Granada and his country, overall. If the roles had been reversed, I could probably give you an overview of US history but my basic knowledge couldn't even come close to the detail that he provided.

Nicaragua is known as the land of volcanoes and lakes but I thought a solid argument could be made for adding churches into the mix. I lost count of how many churches we passed. Some were well maintained, colorful and large while others were older and appeared to be in a state of ruin. I asked Fabian if the run down ones were no longer in use but he assured me that they were indeed still open to the public. In two of the churches, we climbed the stairs to the bell tower. While I loved the views from the bell towers, the narrow, circular stairs and my fear of heights did make my heart beat a little faster.

Each of the churches had an open area outside the front doors. Fabian told me that historically, it was in that area that the indigenous people were required to stand and listen to the sermon, as they were not allowed inside the church. I shook my head as I thought of all of the different cultures that have created a similar dynamic. It hardly seemed like a good conversion strategy to me.

We then walked to the local market, which was similar to a swap meet in the States. People had tables with goods on them and you could buy all manner of things from cheese (not refrigerated, mind you) to deodorant to shoes. There were enormous bins of grains and beans, tables covered in vegetables and beautiful cut flowers. It was a Saturday and the market was full of people.

Fabian knew I was a vegetarian and told me he didn't intend on taking me into the "meat" section. While I thanked him for his consideration, I told him it was something I'd like to see. Being vegetarian was my personal choice but I also understood that meat was a very important part of some cultures and I hoped that through experiencing other people's traditions, I would learn and have a better understanding of this world we share.

The meat section wasn't at all organized like the ones I had no need of in the States. There were pigskins and the faces of pigs (only the front half) as well as many other parts of animals that I won't mention and none of it was refrigerated. I didn't regret my choice to observe their meat practices but it was not an experience that bears repeating. The memories of what I saw will stay in my head for a lifetime but it was really interesting to see what is normal for another culture and to experience how they live their daily lives.

The city roads were all very clean and the center medians were lined with trees. It must have been trash day as there were little tied up bags of trash all along the median. The sidewalks were constructed of different materials and pavers, making unique quilt like patterns.

There were dogs and horses on the sides of the roads and sometimes in the middle (creating a lack of desire to ever drive there), and lots of people were just hanging out, enjoying their Saturday with family and friends in the town square. Two girls were carrying round metal trays on their heads without the aid of their hands and they were overflowing with some type of food.

The city itself was very colorful. The buildings were all painted in bright colors and one could easily pinpoint the Spanish influence. The roofs were made from terracotta tiles and there were large open courtyards in the middle of homes for entertaining. It seemed the main modes of transportation in the city was not the automobile but rather bikes, horse drawn carriages and walking, which of course contributed to the slower pace of life, and it felt so lovely not to rush all the time.

I also saw a man selling several little plastic bags filled with colorful liquid. I knew these were sugary juice drinks from watching an episode of Bizarre Foods with Andrew Zimmern on the Travel Channel a few months before. However, I couldn't figure out how to drink them. There were no cups, yet they were still considered "to go" beverages and it seems like people really enjoyed them.

We ended our tour at a cigar shop as I had a friend who wanted me to bring him back Cuban cigars. I told him unless he wanted to bail me out of jail after being caught by Miami customs agents, I would bring him home Nicaraguan cigars instead. I was impressed with the shop; they made the cigars on the premises and they even offered organic cigars. The cigar maker was not on the premises that day but had he not had the day off, I would have been given a tour and shown how they were made.

I was not impressed by the fact that in their courtyard, they had a scarlet macaw in a cage. Those are endangered birds and while they are beautiful, they are also very large and deserve to able to fly freely in their natural habitat. Actually, all birds deserve freedom, regardless of size but it really crushed me to see the large bird being kept as a pet instead of flying free. I spoke with Fabian about the situation and he told me that Nicaragua doesn't have laws about keeping wildlife as pets. Later, Matt told me that you could drive north in Nicaragua and actually purchase wildlife (such as monkeys) alongside the road. Just as Troy said, Nicaragua was behind Costa Rica in many ways; not just with their horse drawn carriages but also with their animal protection laws. Then again, the United States doesn't have protections either, and certainly considers itself to be advanced. Unfortunately animal cruelty is a worldwide problem and happens in our own backyard, much more than we would like to acknowledge.

That afternoon was the only rain shower I experienced during the day while I was there and it gave me the opportunity to take a few moments to rest and just enjoy the sounds of nature. It did rain at night however and there were also strong winds in the late evening. Nicaragua uses some of their wind to make energy (with windmills on the Lake near the border of Costa Rica) and hopefully, they will continue to build and install more in the future, continuing this positive trend of renewable energy.

The next day Fabian and I went to Mombacho volcano and cloud forest. While usually covered in clouds, on a clear day you could see spectacular views of Lake Nicaragua, its islands, Granada and beyond. Mombacho is a dormant volcano with two main craters. The day I visited, there was a dense fog (hence the name "cloud forest") but it was still lovely and refreshing. Had the sun been out, it may have been too hot to really enjoy the hike.

We entered one field where there were hundreds of wild orchids growing and the trees trunks and branches throughout the forest were all covered in bromeliads. We also saw lots of interesting insects like beetles and centipedes. At one point, Fabian had me place my hand into a small hole in the side of the mountain. I wasn't sure why but once my hand was inside, it was clear it was a "fumarole" from the volcano. Just as in Rincon de la Vieja, there was hot steam being released.

After the hike, we visited a local arts and crafts town and I saw how pottery was made by hand. We also visited a town on top of one of the mountains that had a beautiful view of Granada, Lake Nicaragua and beyond.

That evening, I asked Chef Calley if she could prepare me a few light snacks for my ride to Costa Rica the next day. She was happy to do so and I was so very grateful. I knew it would be a long drive and I wanted to make sure I had a little nourishment on the road. Two of the snacks I'm still thinking about today: a fruit/nut bar and plantain chips. They were both so delicious and I'd love to find a way to recreate them at home. Perhaps one day the Cayuga hotels will produce a recipe book and I can recreate all of their delicious meals for friends.

The next day, traveling to Costa Rica by van, the driver spoke very little English. We drove past vast amounts of open space and even with all of my travels to Costa Rica, I was still surprised, and impressed, at how much open space there was. In California, I sometimes felt like they had pretty much wiped out any natural spaces that once existed in favor of houses, malls and freeways. It was little wonder that mountain lions and bears could be found wandering around the suburbs, as there was nowhere else to go.

As we approached the border, we crossed over into the lane belonging to the oncoming traffic because our own was taken over by 18-wheelers waiting for the opportunity to get through the border. There was also an ox-drawn wagon in the middle of the road but it failed to shock me since I have gotten used to such during my travels.

When we arrived at the border, my driver pointed in the direction of one of several buildings and tried to tell me to go over there to deal with immigration. I gave him a blank stare as there were three buildings in the general direction that he was pointing and I was at a loss to figure out which one he meant. He eventually got out of the van and walked with me which was greatly appreciated. The building he had been pointing to was closed and we had to go in the opposite direction. It was there that a man brought over a police officer to speak to us. Their speech was too fast for me to understand but they then turned to me and I was told to give the officer $10 and I wouldn't have to wait in the long line to get through immigration. I did so wondering if I'd just paid off a Nicaraguan police officer and feeling like quite the rebel woman.

# Chapter 14

*Playa Tamarindo-Tenorio-San Jose, Costa Rica*

It was only about a four-hour drive from the boat dock in Granada to Playa Tamarindo, though it took an additional hour to get through the border and then deal with immigration on the Costa Rican side. There was a heavy rainstorm in the Northern part of Costa Rica and I think that slowed us down as well. My driver was very cautious, rarely passing vehicles on the left when they were going too slow.

Upon arrival in Tamarindo, the plan was to find Alamo Rent a Car, sans an address since that's not how things work there. However, the car I had reserved turned out to be a manual transmission and the rental agency didn't have any automatics, the problem being that I had never driven a stick shift before. Thank the heavens above, my driver was backing out of the parking lot as this was being discussed and I was able to run out the door and into the street to stop him so that he could take me to Capitan Suizo. The representative at Alamo apologized for the confusion and told me he'd have an automatic for me the next day but at least I had a way to get where I needed to go.

To make matters worse, Troy did not bring his luggage to work with him and the absence of a car meant I couldn't take him back to his place to get it. We missed the sunset, which bummed me out, but when he finally arrived shortly after 6:00, it was just like old times. We met in the lobby, gave each other a long hug and instantly, I was reminded of how comfortable our relationship could be. I forgot the headaches from the last six months and could just be present with my love. No worries, no cares. Just love, peace and joy. We walked on the beach and listened to Bob Marley and Steel Pulse (I had to download a new music selection as Bob was getting old). We laughed, smiled and gave each other sweet kisses. His touch was so soft and my heart reopened melting into his.

At the bungalow later that night, I gave Troy a copy of my first book. I thought he would just put it inside his backpack to take home with him but to my surprise, he actually sat down on the sofa with me and read through it, page by page. We talked about each of the photos and since many of them were taken with him, it was a great way for us to reminisce about our travels together over the last three years. I thought it was a sweet gesture on his part to take that time and really be interested in something I had done.

Troy had to work the next day, which gave me a free day to spend in Tamarindo. I ended up going for a walk on the beach as the tide was out and the water looked so glassy and calm. It was still early but the sun was already hot and I decided to sit by the pool and read one of my books. Later, as I was walking up to the lobby to check emails, I saw little Lola in one of the large Guanacaste trees. She hadn't grown much since my visit in November and I could see she was just learning how to hold onto the branches and trunk of the tree with her tail to help her climb and remain balanced. Some of the branches were so wide, she was unable to get her arms wrapped around them and I could see her struggling a little but she was really trying, just as a child does when they are first learning to walk.

I spent the afternoon with Nati, meeting her for a long lunch at Nogui's, one of the oldest beachfront restaurants in Tamarindo. It was so great to spend a few hours with her, catching up. We walked into town to pick up the rental car and then drove back to the hotel where I gave her a copy of my first book as well. I was so excited to share my project with my friends who would truly appreciate it.

Troy mentioned to me the night before that the dirt road leading to Capitan Suizo was going to be paved in the coming months. As Nati and I drove back to the hotel, I told her about my mixed feelings on the issue since it would mean more development was taking place. I remembered the first time on the road with the Almera and knew that paving it would be good for smaller vehicles but I still didn't like the increased construction and traffic, not to mention the decrease of natural habitat and wildlife.

Troy wanted to take me to Playa Conchal, a pristine, white sand beach he loved. We had to drive on other beaches to get there, which was strange but adventurous. Just before sunset he suggested that we go to Playa Brasilito so we drove a few minutes North, stopping first at the market to pick up a few beers. At Brasilito, we found ourselves a piece of driftwood to sit on while we watched the sun go down. There is nothing sweeter than enjoying a beer with your love, on a beautiful beach, watching the sun melt into the horizon with music playing in the background from the car radio. We then drove through the town of Playa Flamingo as it was another beach he wanted to show me and as it was starting to rain, we headed back to Tamarindo for dinner. The lightning show on the drive back was incredible. There is so much open space and clear air in Costa Rica that when lightning strikes, you can see it from miles away. Troy and I both agreed it was spectacular, as long as it wasn't going to strike anyone.

I had been craving pizza and Troy and I decided to try out a new restaurant called "Esquina". It was a brick oven pizza place in downtown Tamarindo, near the dirt road that led Capitan Suizo and Playa Langosta. The owners were a young family from Argentina and they provided a friendly, family style atmosphere in their open-air restaurant. The prices were reasonable and both the food and service were excellent.

Since I was visiting during the week, Troy had asked for a day off from work and we decided to visit Tenorio Volcano and National Park. He had a friend who worked there and we were able to get a private tour. Tenorio is one of those places in which the website that describes the Park doesn't give you all of the details you should know before you go. The main issue is that the road into the park is terrible and if you're in the middle of the wet season, you really should have a 4x4 vehicle. Even Troy, who is really careful when he drives, lost control at one point. Fortunately, he veered the car towards the mountain rather than the cliff. It was about a two hour drive from Tamarindo which was more than I had expected but well worth it.

Tenorio is famous for its Rio Celeste.  The river is a rich, natural blue color (the color is not a reflection like most water). If I understand the science correctly, the color is created by minerals in the water, which originate in the volcano. Both Troy and I were in awe of this beautiful color as we had never seen anything like it. The hike was very muddy, occasionally pulling off my Teva sandals and once sucking me in so badly I had to have Troy help me out. We hiked down to the base of the waterfall and it was just so magical. The water was so clear, so clean. And this time, I did remember to get the panorama shot.

On the way back to the hotel, the GPS died again and we ended up getting lost. I became convinced that the GPS either didn't like heights or the humidity as I had no problems with it at home. Eventually we came across a farmer who confirmed that we were going the wrong way and we got turned back in the right direction. We were rewarded for our efforts when we saw a beautiful rainbow to the east. Every ten to fifteen minutes during the drive Troy would lean over towards me, smile and say, "Un beso" and I would give him a kiss. He drove with just one hand, leaving the other available to hold mine.

As we approached the beach cities, we listened to the surf report on the radio and heard that the surf was up at Playa Grande. Troy called a friend and we met him at Troy's house to pick up their surfboards and head from one beautiful water spot to the next. It's a hard knock life.

Our last morning together, Troy told me that, while in Panamá, I shouldn't talk to any strangers. I laughed acknowledging that if I followed his advice, I wouldn't be able to talk to anyone. This was the first time I didn't have a subsequent trip planned for the future and we wondered when we would see each other again. As we said our goodbyes, he held me close and gave me a long kiss, telling me as usual, "Hasta luego" even though that wasn't certain, merely hopeful.

My days with Troy were different, this trip. There had always been friendship and passion but there was something else this time. He didn't push me away at the end like he normally did. Our connection just continued to develop and grow into such an openhearted and honest love.

Back at the hotel, I stopped by the gift shop where my first book was available for sale. My appreciation for Troy was momentarily overshadowed by the pride of seeing my work on display and the opportunity to discuss its message with the cashier.

## San Jose

There were only five other people on the plane and the employee who checked me in didn't charge me for the extra bag I had with me. As I walked to the plane, a young man asked me, "Tip for watching your bag?" I chose not to give him any money but was surprised that I was approached like that, since it had never happened to me before.

Fortunately, the hotel shuttle was there to greet me and it was a quick drive to the hotel. I immediately called my friends, Silvia and Maureen, as we were going to meet and enjoy a meal. As we pulled down the street where the restaurant was located, I noticed a McDonald's across the street and made a joke about them taking me there. We all laughed and shared the sentiment that fast food, especially McDonald's, was not real food.

Silvia and Maureen had to help me understand the menu before we could order and get caught up on how life had been since I saw them the year before. As we were talking, we experienced an earthquake. Silvia immediately grabbed my arm, dragging me off the bench and telling me to run for the door. Maureen, on the other hand, laughed, thinking that Silvia was totally overreacting. Fortunately, it was just a quick earthquake and didn't do any damage.

I was actually only supposed to be in San Jose for a few hours but the Panamá airport was closed for repairs so I'd had to change my hotel plans and rebook my flight for a 6 a.m. departure. While I wasn't happy to be spending less time in Panamá, I was thrilled that I got to spend an extra forty-eight hours with Troy and I was able to make time to see Silvia and Maureen.

The next morning the alarm went off at 4:15 a.m. It was actually my first good night of sleep (because I was in the city and there were no jungle sounds in the middle of the night) and I was bummed I didn't have a few extra hours. I dragged myself out of bed with a yawn and a building excitement for my first trip to Panamá.

At the airport, I was charged for my extra baggage this time around. I also got selected for extra security measures, including going through my luggage. It's odd though since they have x-ray machines but I didn't think I had a choice. The airline agent went through every single item in my luggage; toiletries, each "day" of my vitamin holder and even my condoms and birth control. I was mortified that all of this was happening where all of my fellow passengers could see. I didn't relish the thought of everyone else knowing my personal business. My personal favorite moment though was when the agent came across my melted zinc vitamin and had to ask several other staff members for confirmation before I was allowed to keep it. I'm not certain what he thought it might do... perhaps keep the plane from getting a proper tan?

As we went through the x-ray machines, the person in front of me (who I believe was from Holland), had two small bottles of insect repellent in his carry on. The security agent said she had to confiscate them per Costa Rican law. The man became upset and was speaking in English to the agent, telling her it's just travel sized repellent. I wondered to myself if they were going to confiscate my hand sanitizer, which the germaphobe in me hoped wouldn't be the case. Eventually, the Dutch man gave up and I got through security without any problems. A few minutes later, the pilot came into the waiting room and told him that he would take the repellent in the cockpit and give it back to him once we arrived in Panamá. Problem solved.

## Chapter 15

Bocas del Toro, Panamá

It was an hour flight to Panamá and when we arrived, the time difference had jumped us ahead one hour. The immigration process consisted of a single woman in an office handwriting everyone's information: passport number, name, location, profession, reason for visit and duration. My bags were inspected, again, out in the open for everyone to see which I was equally thrilled about and from there, I met my driver who took me to the boat dock.

I was so excited to be in Panamá; especially in Bocas del Toro. Troy told me that it was beautiful and that I'd especially love it for my photography work. Unfortunately, unlike my visits to Nicaragua and Costa Rica, I found the people in Panamá to be very unhelpful and somewhat unfriendly. My guides and hotel staff were polite but it felt forced because it was their job.

I was also taken aback by the lack of environmentally conscientious practices by the hotel staff. On a mangrove tour, one of the guides spotted a sloth and the boat stopped so we could look at it. What I didn't realize was the boat driver had hopped off and was climbing up the tree to get the sloth. As he was climbing, he broke the branch the sloth was resting on and the sloth was literally dangling off the tree above the mangled branches of the mangrove. The driver managed to reach down and grab him to hand him over to the guide. At this point, I was completely horrified. The guide knew I was a photographer so he kept asking me if I had gotten the shot while I tried to explain that I thought he should let the sloth go back up in the tree. I wondered just what environmental protections existed in Panamá for wildlife.

Later that afternoon, the chef came to my bungalow as one of the staff members had told him I was a vegetarian. I had emailed the hotel this information but unlike Jicaro, they didn't take it into consideration prior to my arrival. He wanted to make sure he could provide me with delicious meals, which I thought that was an incredibly thoughtful gesture however the food turned out to be awful. For example, a cheese quesadilla came with mozzarella, bleu cheese and orange cheese - it may have even been cheez-whiz. I may have grown up being fed orange "American" cheese, but I was definitely not a fan as an adult, nor did it complement the other cheeses at all. The hotel also offered appetizers before dinner but they turned out to be Milano cookies and the bread at dinner was, no kidding, white Wonder bread. I thought it was all very odd considering the fact that the hotel rates were over $300 per night.

There were some good points about the Bocas trip. I took many amazing photographs of coral, fish and starfish that lived in very shallow waters along one of the beaches. I saw a few wild dolphins and enjoyed swimming in the incredibly warm, blue-green Caribbean Sea. I visited the San Cristobal Island Indian Community and while the population wasn't quite what I had expected, it was still a very small community of native people who lived off the land. Their homes were simple, constructed of old wood, thatched roofs, and without any insulation. Everything they needed was within a two to three minute walking distance for them: the school, the health center, the church, the market and their homes.

They did have some modern conveniences such as electricity, which the government helped them install as well as modern clothes; some of the kids were even wearing US baseball team caps. Most of the younger ones (ages 1-5) just wore undergarments but the older kids were all dressed in shorts and t-shirts and just like kids in the US, in the group shots, the kids in the back made bunny ears over the kids in the front.

With permission of the parents, I took photos of the kids who loved to see themselves on the digital screen. The boys did handstands for me and one of the girls brought out her doll to show me. There were also dogs and chickens running around loose between the homes as well as a piglet that was running around one of the gift shops.

At one point, my guide took a machete (I have gotten used to the rampant use of machetes in Central America) and cut down a stalk of sugar cane to sliced apart so that I could try it. I was amazed at how the sugar that I buy in the store, while ultimately the same product, did not begin to compare.

While at the hotel, I met some very nice people from the US, Cuba, Brazil, Spain and Norway. Two of the people I met were research medical doctors at Brown University. They happened to be on my flight to Panamá City the day I left Bocas so I had an opportunity to learn more about them and the work they do in developing countries.

When they asked me if I had gotten a yellow fever vaccination, I thought they were kidding but they told me Panamá was still considered to have the threat of yellow fever and I should consider getting a vaccination when I arrived in Panamá City. Since I didn't get the vaccination, I worried over every bug bite I got for the next four days, especially since they had told me there was a 40% mortality rate with the disease.

## Chapter 16

Panamá City, Panamá

I flew into the smaller of the two Panamá City airports and found my luggage and driver without any issues. Albrook Airport is located at the entrance to the Canal so my first view of the Bridge of the Americas, Miraflores Lock and the ships waiting out in the Pacific happened in the air, as we were on approach.

My flight arrived at 10 a.m. and while the hotel knew I would be checking in early the receptionist was quite adamant that no rooms were available. This really surprised me since it was a huge hotel and it seemed like there were hardly any people there. There were generally only one or two other couples dining in the restaurant and only a few people hanging out by the pool. But she insisted there were no rooms available and so I waited in the lobby for an hour while they prepared my room.

When I finally did get to my room and began to unpack my carry-on, a little gecko surprised me as I opened one of the side pockets! He was so very cute and also very scared. The poor little guy must have hid in my carry on when I was packing in Bocas and now he's in a brand new town. I found him in the pocket that had my Trader Joe's trail mix and while it was in a Ziploc, I just wonder if he was hungry and trying to get some food. I attempted to get him onto my hand to take him outside but he was so scared that he jumped off and ran under the bed. I didn't see him again but I left the balcony door open and hoped he made new friends and found a new home.

My first tour in Panamá City was to visit the canal and I was so very excited. While I don't believe in what it stands for (excess consumerism and environmental destruction) and I don't like how they're expanding the canal to enable wider ships access, it was really interesting to see this part of history and to reflect on the technology that was used almost one hundred years ago. My guide, Octavio (who was one of the friendlier people I met in Panamá), and I watched as a huge Hyundai container ship waited for the West side of the lock to fill up and become even with the water level on the ship's side. The ship was so large that it almost touched the sides of the Canal as it slowly maneuvered through. There were several little "mules" (small locomotives) that were attached to the ship on each side by a cable to guide the ship and keep it from damaging the edges.

The Canal is fifty miles long and it can take 8-10 hours for a ship to cross through from one side to the other. I was told it costs almost one million dollars per day to manage the Canal (including maintenance, salaries, etc). What I didn't ask, and should have, is how much money is brought in per day by the tolls issued to the ships and boats that pass through. The Canal also employs almost 10,000 people. At the Miraflores Lock, they have a visitor's center and exhibits to learn more about the history of the canal and how the locks work. They even have a virtual computer exhibit that allows you to be the captain of the ship as it goes through the lock!

Visiting Panamá City, Octavio and I drove through both good and bad areas. There was a large police presence (and I also noticed the US Coast Guard when I was in Bocas), which didn't do much to reassure me, but I never felt unsafe. Then again, I did have a driver and wasn't totally on my own. Octavio told me if the police officers were dressed in black, it indicated a good part of the city, but to be wary of the areas where the officers were dressed in green.

I also noticed that the majority of the homes had electrical wires hanging off the sides and front of the buildings. I'm not just talking about one wire that runs the length of the building and is properly tacked up (like a cable or satellite dish wire might be), but multiple wires (10+) that are loosely hung off the buildings and which really seemed like a fire hazard. I brought this to Octavio's attention and he told me that "it's just the way it's done" and there weren't electrical code requirements.

Octavio told me there are people in Panamá from all over the world, mainly because when the US took over the construction of the Canal from the French, the people they brought in stayed after the work was completed. He assured me that none of them were slaves but I did have to wonder.

In both Bocas and Panamá City, many homes had neon pink notices on their front doors. While I had asked my guide in Bocas what they meant, I was simply told that it was for the census. Since Octavio was more personable and talkative, I decided to ask him to elaborate.

Octavio explained that the census (which occurred every ten years, just as in the US) had taken place on Sunday, May 16th. Every person had been required to stay at home in order to be counted. He told me that if you were found outside of your home, you would be asked to show the police officer a special card, acknowledging that you had already participated in the census. If you did not have that card, you would be charged a fine and spend the day in jail. There really wasn't any reason why the people still had the signs on their front doors, other than they just hadn't removed them. While Panamá only has about 3 million people, I was nonetheless impressed that every single person throughout the country was counted in just one day. Octavio told me the majority of people live in one of the two major cities, Panamá City on the Pacific and Colón on the Caribbean.

The next day, I had the opportunity to visit the Smithsonian Tropical Research Institute on Barro Colorado Island. I thought it was funny that I was notified in advance to wear long pants and sneakers or hiking boots. I'd never brought long pants or sneakers/boots for any of my hikes in Costa Rica and neither of those items would fit into my carry-on suitcase that the puddle jumpers required so I ended up wearing shorts and open-toed Teva sandals. My guide, Melissa (another one of the friendlier people in Panamá), told me to watch out for army ants. I felt sure that the Institute's reason for advising that visitors wear long pants and boots was because it was a US owned business and they didn't want to get sued if any ants, scorpions or ticks attacked.

The hike was pleasant (even thought it was almost 100 degrees and humid) and Melissa had plenty of information to provide to us about the flora and fauna as well as the scientific research taking place year round on the island. Barro Colorado Island is just 3,700 acres but there was a wide diversity of inhabitants: over 1,300 types of plants, 300 birds, 35 amphibians, 70 reptiles including 5 venomous snakes, 110 mammals (including 74 types of bats of which we saw two), 200 types of ants, 300 butterflies, and 100 cockroaches. There are also spiders, ticks, chiggers and tens of thousands of other types of insects. She told us jaguars currently swam between the mainland and the island however because of the widening of the canal, they were unsure how that would impact the species in the future. I also learned the spots on an ocelot are like a human fingerprint; no two are the same.

During the PowerPoint presentation, a special credit was given to the man who had installed all of the concrete pavers on the hiking trails throughout the island. That had to have been quite an undertaking since there are over forty-two kilometers of trails (and it's not like they were flat walking trails).

> We so often do not consider the work that goes into creating something, which we can then later enjoy. This doesn't just apply to a situation like this one though; it applies to everything we have in our daily lives: our food, our clothing; all of our "belongings". Someone worked to create each piece for us and I feel like we should take a moment to look around at all that we have and be appreciative, especially since many of the people working to create these things may have not been paid a fair wage or been provided with adequate working conditions.
>
> Reflect on this the next time you purchase food, clothing, coffee, chocolate, diamonds, or really just anything that wasn't made in the US. Then, if you haven't already, search for an alternative where the items carry the Fair Trade label. It might take a little more effort on your part but really, isn't it worth it to be a part of the solution rather than perpetuating the problem?

With the temperature being so hot during the hike, I returned to the hotel, exhausted, took a cold shower and ordered room service. I had no idea how hot Panamá could get. I then turned on the TV for the first time in almost two weeks and was very surprised to find an episode of Bonanza on one of the channels. Generally, I've found that many Costa

Rican stations are one or two seasons behind the US but Bonanza puts us into another generation... or two.

The best part of my trip to Panamá City was my visit with the Embera Indians, an indigenous culture living in a remote area of Panamá. They have no electricity, wash their clothing by hand and they cook over an open fire. They live off the land for the most part and eat the fish in the stream. Next to the underwater coral and starfish photos I took in Bocas, this excursion definitely made the trip to Panamá worthwhile.

We rode in a dug-out canoe to get to their village and our first stop was a hike to a beautiful waterfall. While on the shallow river, we were followed by hundreds of yellow butterflies that looked like they were dancing in the air. After the waterfall, we went to their village where we were welcomed by the Indians who were dressed in their traditional clothing.

They prepared us a meal of fish (which I didn't eat) and patacones (fried plantains) over an open fire along with fresh fruit. The food was then served in a large leaf, creating less waste as the leaf could just be composted and made into mulch when we were done eating. No utensils or plates were needed.

With the help of a translator (as they have their own traditional language and do not speak Spanish), they taught us about their community, history and the arts and crafts they created. They are known for their handicrafts such as traditional, hand-weaved baskets and hand-carved sculptures. I was impressed to learn that each color of the fabric used is made naturally, without chemical dyes. For example, a reddish brown color is made by soaking fabric made of plant parts in water and burying it in the earth for several days. Other dyes, as well as the carvings, come from fruits, nuts and plants in the rainforest. Nothing is ever wasted or taken for granted. They are a traditional people who know how to live with the land, only taking what they need.

After lunch, they performed for us by dancing, chanting and playing music. They even invited us to join in. My favorite moment though, was when I saw three young children (probably between the ages of three and eight), reading a book off to the side of the festivities. It was such a sweet moment to see the one older boy reading the book as the younger two looked on.

Unfortunately, I left my Teva's in the guide's van adding to my tally of items left behind on trips.

On my last day there, I did finally see a "Jesus Christ Lizard" walk on water. He was running across one of the pools at the hotel and the sight lived up to its reputation.

I also saw an Agouti in the hotel's landscaping, eating its breakfast of leaves and dropped fruit. Agouti's are very skittish animals and are a part of the rodent family, I was told. They were very large and unlike other smaller rodents which I imagine will climb trees, I've only ever seen agouti's on the ground.

Driving to the airport the next day, we must have passed at least thirty fast food chains (there were multiples of each) as well as huge banners that were attached to street overpasses announcing the latest deals at Subway, Burger King and KFC. I made a comment about how many there were and my driver told me the fast food restaurants delivered. Not just the pizza places but the burger and sandwich places as well. I was shocked. At least in the US, we had to walk to our cars to get to the restaurants. But in Panamá, you just had to walk to your front door.

The Panamá City airport was much more efficient and technologically advanced than the Bocas airport and I got through security pretty easily except for the woman who kept insisting I put one of the AA paper luggage tags on my bag when I already had one of my own.

I visited the Admirals Club once again (it's free, so why not?) and enjoyed a little quiet time as I waited for my plane to arrive.  As I sat there, watching the planes arrive and depart, I realized just how exhausted I was. I did not have one single day during this trip where I just relaxed on the beach or poolside all day. I really do need to learn how to slow down and actually take a vacation.

Flying over Panamá City and heading East towards the Caribbean, I took one last look out the window at the beautiful countryside and blue-green Caribbean Sea.  Even though I'm departing from Panamá, it is with much sadness that I am leaving the Rich Coast once again and returning to the States. I normally have my next trip planned out before I leave but this time, funds were scarce and I couldn't even begin to think about when my next trip would be much less where my adventures would take me.

In Miami, the customs agent asked, "You went to all of these countries on this trip?  Nicaragua, Costa Rica and Panamá?" He asked me what types of gifts I had bought since I had written it on my customs form.  I don't know why I fumbled for an answer but I couldn't get any words out so he followed up by asking if I was bringing any alcohol, tobacco or firearms into the country. I quickly answered "No" only to realize seconds later that I had just lied.  I had Nicaraguan cigars for my friend.

"Oh my god," I thought, "What if they go through my luggage and assume I deliberately lied?"

I started to panic. I can laugh at it now. However, at the time, I remember sitting in the Admirals Club fearful I would hear my name called over the intercom demanding that I return to Customs.

As we departed Miami and headed West, I chased the sunset home; it was fitting since the sunset signified that the day was over, as was my trip. I arrived in San Francisco just in time to catch the Airport Express to head back to Sonoma County. It was an hour-long ride and while my body was exhausted, I couldn't stop thinking about the sadness I felt leaving Central America; not knowing when my next trip would be was truly disheartening.

While I've always known it, at that moment, I was deeply aware of the connection I have to the Rich Coast and wondered when I would be able to return. I looked out the window but I couldn't see any stars in the night sky. Between the fog and the lights of the city, they just weren't visible. I closed my eyes and thought about the night sky in Costa Rica; the fresh clean air, the absolute darkness and with the exception of the natural world, the peaceful silence.

The taxi dropped me off at my house just after 1:00 a.m. I knew I had about three hours of meowing from my cat ahead of me. As I tried to fall asleep, he pressed the soft pads of his little paws into my face and purred loudly, his way of telling me how much he missed me.

# Chapter 17

*Prelude to Trip 8*

Summer/Fall 2010

I was broke. Completely broke. It was as if I awoke one morning and had no money left in my bank account. I couldn't comprehend how this had happened – with the exception of mandatory expenses like food and mortgage, the only money I ever spent, anywhere, was on traveling. I was missing the Rich Coast terribly and my only connection to it was my emails, phone calls and Facebook chats with Troy. While he always brought a smile to my face, there was also an underlying sadness that I was not there, with him, enjoying the tropical winter he was experiencing. And at this point, with no money in the bank, I couldn't get there no matter how hard I tried

To make matters worse, Northern California didn't have a summer in 2010. It was literally cold and foggy almost every day. Even the deciduous trees were confused, their leaves turning from green to red and yellow in early August. As I watched my beautiful tan from the May trip fade, I became even more disheartened as there was no sunshine to warm my body and brighten my spirits.

My relationship with Troy was beginning to develop more and mid-summer, he sent me the following email:

*Hola hola preciosa todo esta bien por aqui espero que tu estes bien...Esta lloviendo mucho por aqui casi todo el dia llueve especial para estar con usted en la cama..besos...*

It just made me miss him so much more. I wanted to be there with him, lying in his bed, his arms wrapped around me as we listened to the rainfall outside. The windows would be open and the fan turned on, letting the humid air circulate through the room. At this point, I was used to the temperature and no longer had the need for a/c.

Things did not improve as we headed into autumn. Actually, they got worse, even though I hadn't thought they could. First I had to let go of my business, forHarmony.net. While the idea of the business was to promote sustainability, it was, unfortunately, not sustaining me. So I shut down my beautiful website and figuratively closed my business doors.

Then, in October, I received an email that was sent from Troy's email account but didn't really seem to be written by him. It was in the first person but wasn't in his usual tone, and the message, well, it basically said that he was in love with someone else, they had been together for almost 2 years, he was marrying her and that I was to never contact him again. "Vete" is how the email ended which, translated, means "go away". I immediately sent a text message to

Troy's cell phone, asking him what was going on. He wrote me back instantly, explaining that his crazy ex-girlfriend had gotten into both his Yahoo and Facebook account (which explained why I had been deleted as his friend). He told me we would always be together and not to worry. A few days later, we spoke and he told me his ex-girlfriend had gained access to his email account and had deleted all of his emails (new, sent, in the trash) and all of his contacts as well. Troy didn't have a "smartphone" so it was not like all of his contacts were in his cell phone and he could easily back up his phone to his computer. He had lost everything. This kind of behavior seemed so ridiculous to me but then I learned she was only 23 years old and it made a little more sense.

The following week, we started communicating again and every day, Troy would send me an email as soon as he got into his office. With the time difference, he always sent it before I woke up so when I checked my emails, I'd have one from him telling me...Buenos dias, mi amor. He regularly told me he loved me and even though I couldn't be there with him, our daily emails made me feel connected both to him, and to his beautiful country.

He wrote to me often, telling me how he'd like to visit me and possibly move to California. I sent him a few job descriptions I found on Craig's List that I thought he would might enjoy. He practiced English with me and I practiced Spanish with him. We talked about him moving here for a few years and then we would move back to Costa Rica together. It really felt like our lives were intermingling much more than in the past and that there was even something to consider more seriously in the future.

And so it was on a chilly 20 degree morning that I decided I'd have to find a way to return to him and the Rich Coast. I reached out to the friends I had made there and was able to make the trip affordable, and used frequent flier miles to redeem a free flight. I was returning to Costa Rica in just under two months and I was overjoyed. The happiness that was lost in the dismal cold was returning and I knew I'd be defrosting in the warm sunshine with Troy's hand in mine, in just a few short weeks.

## Chapter 18

January 2011

The day had finally arrived. I was returning to the Rich Coast. Troy had made the hotel reservation for our first night together in Liberia and had told me he'd meet me at the airport. For the first time in many trips, I wasn't flying first class but fortunately, I had all three seats to myself on the redeye to Miami and I was able to curl up in a tight little ball and sleep for a few hours. Upon arrival at 4:45 a.m., I decided it would be best to spend the $50 and pay for a one-day pass to the Admiral's Club. I had a five-hour layover and decided a shower and hot coffee would ease the pain of having to travel coach.

As I stepped off the plane in Liberia, I instantly felt the connection to the country again. It was almost 90 degrees and I could literally feel my body begin to thaw. After getting through customs and immigration, I stepped outside to the masses of taxi drivers and hotel shuttles and saw Troy there; waiting for me with a smile on his face, his backpack slung over one shoulder and a (somewhat) cold bottle of Bavaria

Gold for me. As he saw me approaching him, he placed the backpack and beer on the ground and instantly wrapped his arms around me, picked me up and twirled me around. He found us a taxi and we paid the ridiculous rate that the taxis always seem to charge to be driven ten minutes into town to our hotel.

We ordered lunch by the pool and spent the next few hours catching up and just enjoying being in each other's presence again. Later that night, we walked to the town center and sat on a bench in the park, having quiet conversation. There were hundreds of people in the park, doing the same thing, but it was as if none of them existed. The universe slowed down and it was as if we were the only two people there. He'd lean over to give me sweet kisses, sometimes even making the sound "muah!" when he did it, just to add dramatic effect which he knew would make me giggle. He loved making me laugh. He told me how much he loved the color of my eyes and how every time I laughed, they'd light up and sparkle. I rested my head on his shoulder and he held my hand on his lap. All was right with the world again.

We found a local bar/restaurant and had a few beers, dinner and listened to a collection of 80's music videos. We played a game of seeing who could name the artist and title first. We spent hours there, laughing and joking around. Walking back to the hotel room, we took a moment to look up at the night sky...taking in the stars and the full moon that was lighting our path. It was a sweet, romantic night and just what I needed.

But the next day, I awoke with an innate sadness. One that I couldn't explain but I knew things were about to change. Troy had told me when I arrived that he had to deal with some work issues in San Jose and would have to leave our first morning together but would meet up with me a few days later in Tamarindo. While it wasn't the perfect week that I had wanted, I understood, and figured we'd still have the entire week in Tamarindo. He wasn't exactly working at the time (hence why he needed to go to San Jose) so we would have both the days and nights to play together.

The shuttle taking me to Santa Teresa that morning picked us up at the hotel and dropped Troy off in the center of town so he could catch a bus to San Jose. That strange feeling was still with me when we stopped to let him out. Troy told me "hasta luego" and gave me a kiss and I answered him with, "adios". The words just came out that way but that's not how you would normally say goodbye to someone who you'd be seeing in just a few short days. I couldn't explain it but I inherently knew that was something wasn't right.

I let the feeling go as there was nothing I could do about it and settled into my seat, for I knew the upcoming ride would be bumpy and long. Hiberio, my driver, was a really sweet man and we talked for much of the trip. What I found most odd was that the CD he was playing was almost identical to the videos Troy and I had been watching the night before. Ticos' really seem to enjoy the music from the 80's.

He made sure to point out every type of plantation we passed by – mango, banana, melon, watermelon, sugar cane and limes. He also announced every town we drove through. He stopped at several vista points to let me take photos and on a very steep, rocky road, he saw an iguana scurrying past and stopped again so I could take a photo. It probably wasn't the wisest idea since even with 4WD, stopping on a steep, unpaved hill is not really recommended but after spinning the tires a few times, he got it back into gear.

Four and a half hours after leaving Liberia, I finally arrived at Latitude 10 Beach Resort in Santa Teresa. Santa Teresa is located at the southern tip of the Nicoya Peninsula. It's known for its excellent surf and beautiful beaches. While I didn't spend too much time in the town, it seemed to have a lot of ex-pats living there, an interesting blend of surfers and hippies that had infiltrated this once sleepy town.

I was welcomed at Latitude 10 by Adriana and she promptly handed me a delicious and refreshing drink, one that was needed after the long drive. She gave me a tour of the hotel, the beach and my beautiful room. There are five casitas on the property and each one is individually tucked away so it's almost as if you have the entire property to yourself.

The accommodations were luxurious but simple. There was no glass in the windows and therefore, no air conditioning, but being at the beach, the tropical breeze cooled the casitas and provided a deeper connection to nature. One question that I didn't think to ask at the time but am now curious about is whether they've experienced any of the local wildlife getting into the rooms. Being completely open, I could see a squirrel, monkey or bird just deciding it would be a nice place to hang out.

The bathrooms were "open sky" style – meaning you literally took a shower outside. It's one of the most amazing experiences to be outside in nature, the canopy of the trees giving you privacy, except for a few monkeys that may pass by.

After taking a moment to settle in, I walked over to the open-air restaurant for bocas and a beer. The bocas was a lovely meal of freshly made tortilla chips, salsa and yucca. I think one of the main reasons I love Costa Rica so much is because of the food; it's much fresher and there is a variety of fruits and vegetables that I cannot readily find in the States. Silvia, the General Manager, and I conversed during the meal and I was somewhat grateful that I was traveling on my own as it afforded me more opportunities to meet new people.

The rest of my day was spent photographing the lovely grounds with my last moments of sunshine spent at the beach, a few steps away from the lodge. As I walked out to the sand, I was excited to see a few people hovering around a turtle. As I got closer, I realized the large turtle wasn't moving, except when a wave would sweep it closer to shore. The turtle was dead and the people informed me that they saw a fisherman's hook in the front right flipper.

I stayed with the turtle, hoping they were wrong and it had died of natural causes but the enormous turtle was eventually overturned by a crashing wave, flipping it onto its back. There, gouged into the right flipper, was a fisherman's hook and chain.

The turtle was eventually swept onto shore and the tide withdrew. The vultures flew overhead as I stood by it. One even landed within a few feet of me but flew off as I walked towards it. In what were only a few short minutes, the little beach insects and crabs were crawling all over the dead turtle and the vultures continued to circle overhead.

I knew this was the circle of life and that everything that lives must die, feeding other living animals. But with turtle populations decreasing and the green turtle listed on the IUCN threatened species list, it was lamentable to see this beautiful, peaceful creature decay back into the earth. Like me, the green turtles are herbivores. Except when just hatched, they don't eat anything but sea grasses and algae. I wonder how it must have felt – to have that hook gouge its skin. Being so close to the joint, I can only wonder if the turtle was in pain and unable to use its flipper properly.

The next day, on a snorkeling tour, our boat captain told me he was a fisherman. I showed him the photo of the hook and he said it looked as if it was from a long line fishing boat. Probably without realizing it was a turtle s/he had caught, the fisher pulled on the line, yanking the turtle around and causing further damage, eventually killing it, cutting the line and dropping it back into the sea. Had the fisher taken a few extra moments to retrieve the turtle, they could have brought it to a nearby animal rehabilitation center and possibly saved its life.

During my first seven trips, I had the opportunity to see green turtles mate in the Pacific Ocean and lay their eggs in a 2-foot hole, which they carefully dug with their back flippers and now I'd seen them die as well. I hoped someday to be able to see them hatch, crawling out from the sandy birthing ground their mother made for them to scurry to the vast ocean to begin a new circle of life.

It definitely created melancholy in me, seeing this turtle die. The hotel staff covered the turtle in sand, allowing it to gracefully return to the Earth where it was born.

The next day, I awoke to the sounds of the howler monkeys and the crashing waves. It was high tide and it was as if the ocean and the monkeys were competing for who could be the loudest. Every once in awhile, a gecko would chirp in my room, reminding me that big or small, we each have a voice and want to be heard.

Maricela works mornings at the hotel and greeted me at breakfast. We talked about her life here in Costa Rica, where she is from originally and she showed me photos of her lovely children. I love meeting local people and hearing their stories. The night before I had spoken with Adriana who told me about her travels in India and how she was excited about her position at the hotel as sustainability coordinator. Cayuga had recently started managing the property and they were in the process of becoming more eco-conscious throughout the resort.

Later that morning, I traveled to Montezuma for a snorkeling boat tour and to spend the afternoon at Isla Tortuga. It wasn't the same, not having Troy to experience it with, but it was still fun and I made several new friends. The first people I met were from Italy and didn't speak English or Spanish. They were lovely people and we managed to communicate with one another through gestures and my limited Italian. I told them about my travels in Italy and how much I loved their country. Truly, Italy is my favorite country in all of Europe. Italy reminds me of Costa Rica and why I love both countries so much – the food, the people and their culture/lifestyle. I also met people from Argentina, Australia, France, Holland and various parts of the United States.

The day was overcast and there was so much sediment in the water that the snorkeling wasn't all that it could have been. Plus, the volcanic rock of the Pacific just does not compare to the beautiful coral gardens found on the Caribbean side. However, on the way back to the dock, we saw several humpback whales and dolphins playing in the Golfo Nicoya. Whales are such massive living beings and it's such an awesome opportunity to see them in their own environment. Everyone on the boat was excited. First, we'd hear the colossal sound from their blowhole and then we'd see them come out of the water, with their tail being the last thing in the air before diving back into the sea.

The next morning, the sun was shining and I took a short walk on the beach before breakfast. It was only a weekend trip to Latitude 10 but definitely worthwhile. In my last minutes there, Greivin, one of their staff members, saw me with my camera and asked me to follow him. He took me to an enormous bush and inside the middle of the bush was a family of opossums.

These were tiny opossums though; not like the ones that I normally see at home, more often than not as roadkill. There was a mom and a tiny little baby whose eyes were just barely open. It was one of the sweetest moments of the trip. A new life had begun.

There had been some confusion with the shuttle company and I asked Adriana to confirm my 10:30 pick up the night before. It turned out the company had forgotten about me and thought I was part of a larger group leaving at 7 a.m. from a different hotel. Fortunately, the shuttle was there, on time, and I returned to Tamarindo, so excited to see Troy and spend the week with him there.

When I arrived at Capitan Suizo, I was greeted by all of the same people who I've known for many years now. Going to Tamarindo is like coming home for me. The only thing I didn't like to see was the overwhelming amount of development occurring and how that was impacting the environment. I still believe we can find a sustainable balance between growth and simplicity; I just hope we find it before it's too late.

Vinicio, the General Manager, came out of his office to welcome me and give me a big hug. The hotel has an unadvertised, very basic room, which he had offered to me and I was grateful he could accommodate me for the week. Troy and I really only needed a place to sleep and shower as our days would be spent outside at the beach and walking around town.

Vinicio told me that the original three orphaned monkeys, Alice, Sophie and Maggie, had been released to Sibu Sanctuary and I was overjoyed to hear that my sweet little monkeys would be taken care of by people I know and admire. What a small world. Capitan Suizo was still caring for Lolita and Linda, both still babies, but their hope is that they too will integrate themselves into one of the many troops that pass through the hotel's natural environment every day or be released into a setting like Sibu.

I mentioned to him that one of the reasons for this visit was to look for apartments for when I permanently move to Tamarindo. He told me he has a small apartment building just outside of the center of town and would be happy to show me one of the available rentals. While I probably wasn't going to move for at least a year, I was excited to see what was available and felt so much more comfortable renting from someone I knew and who would be able to help me adjust to the transition.

Troy wasn't at the hotel when I arrived so after settling into my room, I called him. His mom answered his cell phone and I was once again overcome by that overwhelming feeling of sadness. His mom still didn't speak any English but I knew enough Spanish to discern what she was telling me. After Troy had left me on Friday, he went to San Jose and as he was crossing the street, an oncoming bus hit him. He was transported to a local hospital and was in critical condition for several hours but didn't make it. His wounds were just too severe. I remembered driving in the crazy streets of San Jose one night after leaving a bar with Troy and how no one paid attention to stop lights, stop signs or, for that matter, pedestrians.

My body felt like it was melting into the floor beneath me. I remember sitting down on the bed, in complete shock, hoping that I was hearing her wrong, or that I wasn't getting the translation correct. My heart was racing in my chest and felt so very heavy. While his mom had hung up the phone several minutes before, I was still holding it, just slightly away from my head. I couldn't move. I couldn't do anything. I just sat there, for hours. And then I started to cry. My heart went from feeling heavy to feeling shattered into millions of pieces. I felt empty, sad, devastated and angry. I was overwhelmed with emotion. Here I was, in the most beautiful place on Earth, waiting for my love who would never return.

I really didn't know what to do, at that point. I considered changing my flight and going home the next day. Other than my first cat, I'd never really had to experience death in my life. I'd never lost anyone that I loved so much. I eventually fell asleep that night and the next morning, took a sunrise walk on the beach. The warm sun rising over the immense Guanacaste trees reminded me to be open, to be heart-centered and to be mindful. Later that day I wrote Troy a letter. I knew he would never read it, but there were things that were never said, or just not said often enough, that I needed him to know. I expressed how grateful I was to have him in my life these last four years and for how he taught me so much about life and love and was there to hold my hand in both celebratory and difficult times. I told him I would miss him and that he would always be in my heart. I told him I loved him.

For the most part, the next few days were spent in quiet meditation. I took walks on the beach, enjoyed the troops of monkeys that would pass by my bungalow and tried to let go of the heartbreak I was experiencing. At times, I wished I had a shell, like the hundreds of hermit crabs I had seen at the Latitude 10 beach. I just wanted to tuck myself under the shell and hide there.

The next night, I had dinner at the hotel and while sitting at the bar, I met Calvin, the owner of Los Altos de Eros, a luxury hotel situated up in the hills above Tamarindo. He told me that besides the amazing accommodations, their spa was not to be missed. Oh, how I wished at that moment I had the extra funds to spend on a day at the spa. I desperately needed someone to massage out all the pain, taking away all my cares. But there were no extra funds on this trip so I was left with the tropical warm water of the Pacific to heal the tearful melancholy being felt throughout my body, mind and spirit.

It was the next afternoon that I decided to go on a "catamaran boat and sunset snorkeling tour". I thought it might give me some solace, being out at sea, watching the sunset over the vast sea. What I didn't realize was that this particular tour was a party boat tour: lots of people, lots of alcohol. The first hour or so, I spent going between the quiet space in my head and talking to a lovely couple from Colorado who happened to be staying at Capitan Suizo as well. However, as the day progressed (and the beers were consumed), I let go a little more and started chatting with more people, experiencing a few moments of relief from the despair of the last few days.

One of the crew members, Ryan (again, I cannot understand why I always meet Tico's with non-Latin names) had this amazing smile and when he smiled at me, I couldn't help but smile back. As if there was kismet or some other force working, the next day I would run into him on the beach. He told me he might go surfing later that afternoon but was on his way to work on his dad's boat. While, in any other circumstance, he would have been fun to have a flirtation with, I wasn't in the right mindset to get involved with anyone in that moment.

With fate working in my favor, a few days later as I sorted through my photos I noticed that he was one of the many surfers I photographed one night at sunset. I had given him my business card at the end of the boat tour and after I had returned to the States, he kept in touch and I sent him the photos. He confirmed it was him in the photos and really seemed happy to have pictures of him surfing.

On my last night there, I met a group of people who, as it turned out, visited Tamarindo every year in January. They were fun, and instantly made me feel welcome in their group. We ate breakfast together the next day and exchanged contact information. I told them I hoped to be living in Tamarindo by next January and if that was the case, I'd meet up with them for a meal at the hotel.

I felt so blessed that at such a dark time in my life, I was able to meet so many people who brought love and light to me. However, I had eighteen hours of travel ahead of me that day and the silent flight home was difficult. I spent much of the time just staring out the window. It seemed zoning out over the Atlantic Ocean was easier than closing my eyes, having the darkness surround me as tears rolled down my face.

In the days and weeks since, I have kept in touch with all of the wonderful people I met. I have had numerous opportunities present themselves to me, including the awesome opportunity to live and work in Costa Rica. The loss of Troy has been heartbreakingly difficult but I will always have the memories of our travels and our time spent together these last few years.

The future horizon is brightly lit with much possibility and I know I will love again. My heart is open, my spirit is free and I'm ready to begin the next beautiful stage in my life. As James Dean said, "Dream as if you'll live forever. Live as if you'll die today." That was how Troy chose to live his life, for better or worse. He was a man who truly lived in the present moment; always living for today. Given the events of the last few weeks, that has so much more meaning for me now.

# Epilogue

So, you may ask, after having vicariously traveled with me on eight trips to the Rich Coast, what is in store for me now? Will I travel to other countries like I did on Trip #7 or will my focus remain on Costa Rica? Well, there is still so much more to explore and discover on the Rich Coast. Having suffered the loss of Troy, I recently reexamined my love of Costa Rica…Was it just Troy that brought me down there, year after year, or was it something else? In searching my heart, I realized that my connection to Costa Rica is much deeper than just a love affair with a man. It is an ongoing love affair with a country… its land, people, wildlife, culture, food and overall beauty…and that's not something you can easily let go of. Mi corazón está en Costa Rica. I have a beautiful life in Northern California but Costa Rica will always be where my heart is. I have made wonderful friends there, and I wake up each morning missing the howl of the monkeys, the afternoon rain showers and the billions of stars in the night sky.

I do someday want to travel to other countries: Galapagos, Bali, Antarctica, Cuba, the Maldives and Bora Bora to name a few. For now though, I'm quite content to continue visiting the Rich Coast and creating new memories there.

I want to wake up to the sun rising over the Caribbean Sea and on the same day, watch the sun set over the Pacific. It is possible to do; both by plane or car (plane would be preferable though so as to not waste an entire day traveling). Troy always wanted to take me to hike Chirripo which is Costa Rica's tallest mountain. Recently, my friend, Maureen, mentioned that she wants to hike Chirripo so someday I will go with her. I'm sure I will feel Troy's presence with me as I hike to the summit and take in its magnificent view. I still want to visit the Ecolodges' El Silencio and Morgan's Rock in Nicaragua, and explore the areas where they are located. Poas volcano has eluded me twice now and I am determined to get to that volcano one day! I also want to visit Tortuguero during turtle season, visit a cacao (chocolate) farm, and return to several of the places I've already been such as Manuel Antonio, the Osa Peninsula and Fortuna.

While my goal is to permanently move there in 2012, until then, I enjoy my plantains and gallo pinto with Lizano sauce on top. I keep my GPS set on the metric system so I can learn it better and hopefully not drive down any more one way streets. My home is a gallery of photographs from my travels there and really, all I have to do is close my eyes and I can be in my happy place…where the tropical sunshine warms my body, mind and spirit; connecting me to the awesome world we live in and creating a sense of lighthearted bliss to take with me throughout each day.

*Pura Vida*

# Resources

As I tell my students and clients, there's no need to jump into the deep end first. Taking small steps will enable you to incorporate change into your daily life without it feeling like you have to change everything about yourself. In no time at all, you won't even remember what it was like to respond to the question, "paper or plastic" because you'll already have your own reusable bag with you.

Listed below are resources and recommendations for topics I mentioned in the book:

## Hotels/Retreat Centers

Samasati: www.Samasati.com
Harmony Hotel: www.HarmonyNosara.com
Hotel Capitan Suizo: www.HotelCapitanSuizo.com
Arenas del Mar: www.ArenasDelMar.com
Finca Rosa Blanca: www.FincaRosaBlanca.com
Lapa Rios: www.LapaRios.com
Punta Islita: www.HotelPuntaIslita.com
Jicaro Island EcoLodge: www.JicaroLodge.com
Latitude 10 Resort: www.Latitude10Resort.com
Cayuga Collection of Hotels: www.CayugaOnline.com

## Sustainability

www.Ecotourism.org
www.SustainableTravelInternational.org
www.NatureAir.com (carbon neutral air travel)
www.NativeEnergy.com (carbon offsets)
www.RAN.org (Rainforest Alliance Network)

## Vegetarian/Veganism

www.GoVeg.com
www.PETA.org
www.JoyousVegan.org
www.CompassionateCooks.com

## Fair Trade

TransFair USA: www.TransFairUSA.org
Global Exchange: www.GlobalExchange.org
Brilliant Earth Diamonds: www.BrilliantEarth.com
Fair Trade Resource Network:
www.FairTradeResource.org

## Non-profit organizations

Earth Equilibrium: www.EarthEquilibrium.org
Farm Sanctuary: www.FarmSanctuary.org
Nature Conservancy: www.Nature.org
Nosara Wildlife: www.NosaraWildlife.com
Oceanic Preservation Society: www.OPSociety.org

A portion of the net profits will benefit the following organization:

**Earth Equilibrium:** Equilibrium engages schools, communities, and organizations in transformative educational projects to advance sustainable ways of living with our Planet. We believe that a good life is one where people and nature co-exist in balance with each other.

Our work increases awareness to and engenders a respect for the natural world and the use of its resources. This increased awareness and respect help us understand how we can live more harmoniously with the Earth.

**Our Mission:** To establish a more harmonious way of living within our natural and built environment, while implementing and supporting educational projects that encourage sustainable community development.

**Our Vision:** We envision pristine places where fresh air, healthy soil, and clean water reflect dedicated environmental stewardship.

We imagine places where all people respect nature, find economic value in conserving bio-diverse resources, and believe in the restoration of native habitat. We see places that celebrate a cultural heritage dependent on sound environmental practices. We visualize a Good Life means people and nature are in balance, not at the expense of the natural environment.

*About the Author*

Chrissy Gruninger loves to teach others about our precious planet by connecting inspiring words with beautiful photos. Her intention is to reflect the harmony, the oneness, in all that exists. Through photojournalism, she shares an appreciation and understanding of the natural world, providing the viewer with a glimpse of the extraordinary beauty that surrounds us each day. She lives an intentional, meaningful life; one that is in service to others, providing a voice for those who cannot speak up for themselves.

She is a yoga teacher, health coach and received her Graduate Degree in Integrative Health and Sustainability from Sonoma State University in 2008. In 2012, she followed her bliss and moved to Costa Rica. She owns Social {media} Wellness, a boutique online marketing firm.

To further explore ways on how to live An Intentional Life, one that embodies conscious and mindful action, please contact the author at connect@socialmediawellness.com. Her Living Well Book Series and Rich Coast Experiences Collection are available in print or via download. These books are designed to teach you to live more intentionally; to experience and become aware of the beauty that is within each of us and all that exists in the world.

Made in the USA
Las Vegas, NV
01 May 2024

89380876R00125